Praise for
Stories I Might Regret Telling You

"With disarming candor and courage, Martha tells us of finding her own voice (one, in my opinion, without peer) and peace as a working artist and mother. Her story is made more unique because of the remarkably gifted musical family she was born into."

—Emmylou Harris

"What a wonderful gift this book is! Martha Wainwright has opened the doors and let us into the fabled, glamorous family that is the McGarrigle-Wainwrights. The ups and downs of a family that lives on the stage are shown in all their backstage squalor, and they are even more magical and cruel than one could possibly imagine. Martha shows us what it is like to be the black sheep of the family, the glorious, earnest underachiever who has always been the most loveable of the bunch. Her warm, rich writing displays the same oversharing sweetness that her songwriting possesses; at the same time, it's filled with the humor, panache, and gutsy feminism of her live performances. Martha Wainwright was born in a circus and shows us the great, absurd expectations that come with that birthright. But even more, this book offers a portrait of a modern, blended family that will make you understand and forgive yours. Wainwright shows how a big, dysfunctional brood can be a blessing, filled with surprising gifts that make the heart grow bigger. A surprising and brilliantly relatable book."

—Heather O'Neill, bestselling author
of *The Lonely Hearts Hotel*

"A beautiful and clear-eyed memoir, full of music, friendship, love, and heartache. Somehow at once sizzling and wise, as undeniable as the singer who wrote it."

—Sean Michaels, Scotiabank Giller Prize–winning novelist and founder of Said the Gramophone

"I have been listening to Martha Wainwright for at least twenty years, admiring her from afar. Her new memoir, *Stories I Might Regret Telling You*, made me feel like I was sitting in a corner of one of her New York apartments, reading her private diaries under a blanket with a flashlight. Martha writes like a soldier in the trenches sending word home, not knowing whether she will live or die, bringing uncomfortable, sometimes unbearable, honesty to bear. I was sucked in from the first page, though occasionally I winced because it was all so relatable. A casual sadness strings itself through her story of becoming herself, taking no prisoners, casting regret aside like a cigarette. I kept rereading certain sentences, thinking they would make such wonderful songs. This entire memoir is a song.

"I turned the last page and felt like I had made a new friend, the kind you wish you were cool enough to have but never had the courage to pursue. My only disappointment? Her memoir wasn't long enough. I can't wait for volume two."

—Jann Arden, singer, songwriter, TV star, bestselling author

Stories
I Might
Regret
Telling
You

Stories I Might Regret Telling You

A Memoir

Martha Wainwright

hachette
BOOKS

NEW YORK

Jacket design by Amanda Kain
Jacket photograph © Carl Lessard
Jacket copyright © 2022 by Hachette Book Group, Inc.

Hachette Books
Hachette Book Group
1290 Avenue of the Americas
New York, NY 10104
HachetteBooks.com
Twitter.com/HachetteBooks
Instagram.com/HachetteBooks

First Hachette Books Edition: March 2022

Published by Hachette Books, an imprint of Perseus Books, LLC, a subsidiary of Hachette Book Group, Inc. The Hachette Books name and logo is a trademark of the Hachette Book Group.

The Hachette Speakers Bureau provides a wide range of authors for speaking events.

To find out more, go to www.hachettespeakersbureau.com or call (866) 376-6591.

The publisher is not responsible for websites (or their content) that are not owned by the publisher.

Print book interior design by Abby Reilly

Library of Congress Cataloging-in-Publication Data
Names: Wainwright, Martha, 1976– author.
Title: Stories I might regret telling you : a memoir / Martha Wainwright.
Description: First Hachette Books Edition. | New York : Hachette Books, 2022.
Identifiers: LCCN 2021046685 | ISBN 9780306924682 (hardcover) | ISBN 9780306924675 (ebook)
Subjects: LCSH: Wainwright, Martha, 1976– | Wainwright, Martha, 1976—Family. | Singers—Canada—Biography. | Singers—United States—Biography. | LCGFT: Autobiographies.
Classification: LCC ML420.W125 A3 2022 | DDC 782.42164092 [B] —dc23
LC record available at https://lccn.loc.gov/2021046685

ISBNs: 9780306924682 (hardcover), 9780306924675 (ebook)

Printed in the United States of America

LSC-C

Printing 1, 2022

To my dad and his sister Teddy,
born Martha Taylor Wainwright,
1947–2020

Contents

CONTENTS

One

I WAS BORN MARTHA GABRIELLE WAINWRIGHT in New York State in 1976. My mother, Kate McGarrigle, and my father, Loudon Wainwright III, loved me—or at least they grew to love me. Loudon told me when I was a teenager that he didn't want me at first and pressured my mother to have an abortion. My mom freaked out just as the procedure was about to start, though, and the doctor spoke up. He was concerned for her and he pointed out that Loudon and Kate were married, had some degree of financial stability, and had one child already, my brother, Rufus. Maybe not the best reasons to bring a child into the world, but I'm glad the doctor opened his mouth.

I was surprised when Loudon told me this story, and it also hurt my feelings. I had always felt a little out of place in the world, and knowing that I'd only just barely made the cut didn't help matters any. Perhaps he should never have told me. I don't think my mom would have. When I asked her about it, she said that he had given her an ultimatum. Something like "the baby and me or else the baby and the career but not all three." I never understood why exactly, but perhaps Dad felt threatened by her remarkable talent and didn't like the attention she was getting from record labels at the time. My mother was beguiling and a force of nature and maybe it was all too much for him. I suppose I could ask him about it again, but I don't want to. Kate is not around to hear his answer, and anything he says may be the truth as he sees it but will not be the whole story.

My parents separated anyway, only months after my birth, and my mother carried me and my brother back to her native Montreal. Decades later, I had to navigate a bad divorce myself, and found that being able to explain or express in an exact way how things go wrong is impossible. Their marriage, like mine, was rocky, and now I understand, better than when I was a teenager, why I almost wasn't born.

Montreal is where I grew up, but my brother and I would visit our father and his side of the family in New York three or four times a year and over the summer holidays. We would travel on Eastern Air Lines with our names hung around our necks, chaperoned by what was still referred to as a stewardess. Other times, Kate drove us down, along the Taconic State Parkway.

We spent some of those summer visits on Shelter Island at the eastern tip of Long Island. I always felt like an island myself, and Rufus and I spoke French to each other sometimes so as not to be understood by our father. I have spent my life traveling between these two cities, New York and Montreal, and have never felt fully at home in either, which has suited me fine because I was taught to be an outsider. An outsider with a ferociously close family.

* * *

For better or worse, music is the family business. My mother and her sister performed as the duo Kate & Anna McGarrigle. My father is a witty, morbid songwriter. Rufus is one of the most famous singers in the world, at least in my mind (and his). My half sister, Lucy Wainwright Roche, and one of my father's sisters, Sloan, are singers, too. My cousin Lily Lanken, Anna's daughter, has sung with me for years, but she won't commit full-time to music because she knows what the performing life can do to someone. She and her brother, Sylvan, have designed and stuffed my CDs, driven me to gigs, and helped my career in other ways since the beginning. My ex-husband, Brad Albetta, played bass for me, as well as for the rest of the family. My aunt Teddy, Dad's sister, managed most of us at one point or another, and for twenty years, my other aunt, Jane, managed her sisters, Kate and Anna.

On my father's side, we are related to the Stuyvesants, early settlers of New York, so in my veins runs a diminished WASPy tint of blue blood that has been diluted with Irish and French Canadian red. My mother and her sisters were brought up Catholic. I was never baptized, although I went to a French school and was taught by nuns who told me that I was going to burn in hell with all the other sinners. Rufus loves the WASPy side of the family with its ties to old money (or maybe he just loves money—he has admitted to having a spending problem). But he also loves his Catholic side. His apartment is filled with Virgin Marys and he's always running around the world lighting candles in cathedrals. I don't know if anyone is listening to his prayers, but it seems as though someone could be. I myself admit to having lit a few candles in the last ten or so years of childbirth, death, and divorce. Clearly, the results have been mixed. I don't know what I believe and that's been a problem my whole life.

When I was growing up, my maternal grandmother, Gabrielle, known as Gaby, was my greatest hero. She was old even when I was a baby, having been born herself in 1904; her husband, Frank, was born in 1899. It seemed like a parlor trick to have a grandparent from the 1800s. Gaby was the eldest daughter of a large French Canadian family. Her mother gave birth to seventeen children, and twelve survived. A woman having so many pregnancies always seemed like another parlor trick to me, too, an implausible leftover from a much earlier time.

Gaby was a big part of my upbringing. On weekends and holidays, my mother took us to stay with her in Saint-Sauveur-des-Monts, a small skiing village north of Montreal; when she toured, Gaby took care of us. My grandfather, Frank McGarrigle, had bought an acre of land in the village and, with the help of an architect friend, built the family home and eventually added four small cabins. After he died in 1965, Gaby stayed on in the house we call St. Sauveur—"Saint Savior" in English. Everyone in my family still counts on the place to welcome us and comfort us and smooth us over whenever we're feeling down. Today the house is sinking into the ground— perhaps my grandfather could have used an engineer, not an architect. Most of us have been too busy to deal with it, but recently my cousins did a beautiful thing, rebuilding the living room exactly to the original design and securing at least that part of the house. To me, St. Sauveur is a living thing, almost like a grandmother's lap—a comfortable place you know won't be around forever, so you want to enjoy it while you can. My mother and her sisters grew up there, and Gaby lived there for sixty-odd years, over half of them without her husband.

I loved the stories she told me of 1920s and '30s Montreal. She worked for Marconi as a telephone operator and also as a secretary for the Bronfman family, who were big bootleggers during Prohibition and later built a business empire on the proceeds. As the eldest of so many brothers and sisters, she never wanted to get married and have children of her own. She often told the story of how as a teenager she would sit at the top of the stairs reading her book and as different siblings ascended the stairs to come play or fetch something she would systematically kick them back down. Of course, she did have children, or I wouldn't be writing this, but not until her late thirties. My mother, Kate, was her last, born in 1946 when Gaby was forty-two.

As a grandmother, Gaby wasn't sweet or mean, but some-times she could be both. She had a hunched back, the curve caused by never wearing the special shoe that was supposed to compensate for the fact that one of her legs was shorter than the other. But even with that hunch, she was handsome and strong, and she lived to the age of ninety-one, longer than most of her siblings. She didn't get stuck in her ways but changed with the times; she went from wearing bloomers as a teenager to a T-shirt of my brother's that said "fuck school, fuck work, fuck the president…" in her eighties. She let time have its way with her body, too. Once, she left her false teeth on a table and my dog stole them and buried them in the lawn somewhere. Back to the earth.

The intimacy she shared with me made me feel good. I liked to watch her wash at the bathroom sink and apply moisturizer to the scaly skin on her legs and arms, or muscle cream to her misshapen back. We often slept in the same room and sometimes in the same bed, sharing candies she stashed under it in a plastic bag. I mixed her many gin and tonics, and after I turned thirteen, she let me smoke with her from time to time—neither of us inhaled. I was sixteen when she died, and I felt her presence rise in me so strongly it seemed as if I could take on some of her traits—strength, wit, resilience. But I didn't have her confidence, so I couldn't really pull it off. I simply had to be me, whoever that was. I didn't know for a long time, and maybe still don't.

There were way more women than men in my life as a child, though for ten years we lived with our mom's boyfriend, Pat Donaldson, a bass player from Scotland who had toured with the McGarrigles in Europe. He was tall and handsome, and he always made me feel safe. Kate wrote a beautiful song about Pat called "Stella by Artois." It starts: *Rotterdam '77 I had a birthday…and the boys in the band gave me a candle…and I let you light it for the first time that night.*

Soon after Pat and my mom got together, she bought a rambling old Victorian house in Westmount, a fancy Anglo neighborhood in Montreal. She got it for a song, housing prices having crashed after the first separatist government was elected in Quebec in 1976 and some of the province's English speakers moved out of its jurisdiction. We really stuck out in that upscale neighborhood. It wasn't quite like we were the Beverly Hillbillies, but we were different. Pat's voice was loud and his accent very apparent. He would garden for hours in front of the house, jumping up intermittently to yell profanities at cars that blew through the nearby intersection: "Slow the fuck down, there's a bloody fucking stop sign!"

He also wore the most outlandish clothes. My mother was a great and eccentric dresser, but Pat took the cake. When a production of the opera *Aida* came to Montreal, the cast included elephants and other live animals, so Pat drove the old station wagon to the Olympic Stadium, in his clown pants and oversized colorful beret, to collect the elephant dung for the garden. He was a sight to behold. (Pat later ended up in the circus, working as a bass player and clown, which is just one or two degrees from where my family always stood. We applaud any and all eccentricities.)

But the air between my mom and Pat could be strained, because she was also sometimes his employer, too. This was a dynamic I came to know well, and another thing I have in common with my mother, given that the man I married also played bass for me. Relationships are hard enough without the two people working together, especially when the woman is the boss and the main breadwinner. No matter how things have changed, that role still seems tough on male egos, as if it is the woman's fault that she is making more money.

Thinking back on it now, I realize Pat had an aura of sadness about him, or maybe it was sheepishness, or even guilt, given that he'd left his wife and small child back in England when he'd taken up with my mother. Rufus remembers Kate and Pat arguing a lot; she had the reputation of being a little difficult with the men in her life, which I think was because she was always opinionated and never hesitant to pass judgment. But Pat took good care of me and Rufus, and he was very good at doing and making things: sewing, knitting, woodwork, gardening. He was also a great cook.

I remember a lot of joy when I was a little kid. There were always lots of interesting people showing up at our big house, which seemed bigger, of course, because we were small. The crowd at our place was certainly different from what was going on in the other houses on the block. There were always musicians with their folkie instruments, and characters from my mom and aunt's songwriting past, like their French translator, who had studied French poetry and chemistry at the Sorbonne and was now a struggling dairy farmer with missing fingers. When he came to town, he always brought with him the fresh and strong scent of cow shit, which I liked and didn't like at the same time.

Anna would come to visit, too, from the 250-acre farm where she and her husband, Dane, lived with their two kids. It had been a working farm, but it wasn't anymore. She and my mom had their keyboards set up in our basement, and they made some great music down there with Pat, using lots of synthesizers and looped drum tracks. They had made three successful studio records, one after the other, when we were young, but once we moved into the big house in Westmount, Kate and Anna didn't release another album for eight years.

It was lucky that other singers, like Emmylou Harris, Linda Ronstadt, and Nana Mouskouri, all sang Kate and Anna's songs. And why wouldn't they? The songs—"Heart Like a Wheel," "Goin' Back to Harlan," "(Talk to Me of) Mendocino," and so many others—are amazing. Kate would say to me, "Those women put you through school," and in some ways Emmylou and Linda did feel like other moms. On *Trio*, the 1987 album they made with Dolly Parton, they covered "I've Had Enough"; I spent many hours playing with the cutout paper dolls that came with the LP's deluxe package. They were the women who were out in the world, doing the hard work and reminding people, night after night, song after song, that women are as compelling and creative as men.

My mother would have liked to work more, I think, but a duo is a duo. Anna was reluctant and liked the country life she was living with Dane and the kids. Kate was the more restless of the two sisters. She must have felt extremely torn. She and her sister walked away from a potentially big career right when they started, though whether it was because of their children or their own hardheadedness, I can't say.

By snubbing the music industry, Kate and Anna became more appealing in some ways and in some circles. They also saved themselves from the risk of being chewed up and spat out. I always thought it was weird that my mother, who was such a good performer and singer, never played a show on her own. By the time I was in my late twenties, I had been applauded, lambasted, accepted, rejected, and accepted again ten times over, or at least that's how it felt. I played more shows than Kate ever had and could pick up a guitar and do a ninety-minute to two-hour show anywhere if I had to. Unlike the McGarrigles, I subjected myself to criticism nightly.

The way the sisters approached music was always different from others in their generation. They were young teenagers when they first started playing traditional and old-timey music, but it wasn't until they were in their thirties that they came out with their first record, titled simply *Kate & Anna McGarrigle*. It was met with huge critical praise and won them many fans.

Kate and Anna were stunning, enigmatic, very talented, and charmingly aloof. They were especially successful in Europe, where they would tour a couple of times a year, but they would always come back home to their kids. Their dedication to their home life often meant they cancelled tours and backed out of promotion. Though I do remember one long trip Kate and Anna and their band took to Australia and Hong Kong, when they left Rufus and me in the care of Jane's kids, Anna, who was seventeen, and Vinnie, who was fifteen. My grandmother had to take over after the police came to the door because my cousin Vinnie had been caught shoplifting a bag of potatoes. He had spent all the food money Kate had left for us on cigarettes and a tattoo. Anna's kids, Lily and Sylvan, are only a couple of years younger than me and, once we were all school age, Kate and Anna also played summer folk festivals and brought us along. There are lots of pictures of us caught up in the cables at the front of the stage, looking bored or half singing along in the summer heat. These shows were work, but they were also our summer vacations and usually so laid-back, you could practically imagine a barbecue set up onstage along with some lawn chairs.

I understand what my mother was wrestling with, because I face the same temptation. I have always found it hard to be away from my kids when I'm on the road, and sometimes I think about getting a job in Montreal so I don't have to travel. I fantasize about becoming a checkout person at the Supermarché PA—the groovy grocer around the corner. The idea of clocking in and then leaving your work to go home is very appealing, but then again, playing Carnegie Hall is also appealing.

At home in Montreal, Rufus and I played outside for hours with the other kids from the street. We traveled as a pack, trolling our nice neighborhood, and we always ended up on Army Hill, the grounds of an old military school that had been shut down. We would climb under the fence and play chevalier. Rufus was the knight and I was Guinevere or something. He was always saving me, his princess, then turning around and dunking my head in the poopy birdbath in the old arbor.

He tortured me when we were young. I was told that when my parents brought me home from the hospital, he poured grape juice on my head. He stuck his foot out to trip me as I ran down the hall, he pulled my hair, and he pinned me down and wrestled me. But he has never let go of the one time he says I tried to kill him. We lived on a steep hill, and next to our house were stairs leading to the street above. Rufus is convinced that once when we were playing at the top of the stairs, I intentionally tripped him. He fell and ended up with a bunch of stitches in his head. I only faintly recall the incident, and I'm not sure if it was an accident or if I did it on purpose. Maybe a bit of both. But that's typical of us. We remember things differently and feel them differently, too. My brother was really annoying, but I also looked up to him. This remains the same.

At some point, things between my mother and Pat went sour, and they broke up. I'm sure she loved him, but she was restless. The lack of a full musical life may have played a part, too, but there was also the fact that Gaby had never approved of Pat because he had abandoned his family for her daughter. She pressured my mother to leave him—at least that was the story I always heard. But I never really knew for certain what happened with Pat. It all just seemed like rumors. Then again, I don't know if any man could have pleased my mother enough for him to last. Kate never talked much about the situation. Once Pat left, she must have been lonely, but she was proud, too, and she stood by her decision.

By that time, Rufus and I were changing, too. Rufus, at thirteen, was already expressing his sexuality. This was surprisingly hard for my mother. I was never a hundred percent clear what brought things to a head, but from what I understand, Kate noticed that a man in a car sometimes sat outside our house at night. She also found a pile of gay magazines that I guess freaked her out, because Rufus was so young.

She decided that the best response was to get him out of the city entirely, and she sent him to a boarding school called Millbrook in Dutchess County, the nice horsey part of Upstate New York—a place with a strong theater department and lots of girls. I don't think she really believed the school would change him, but Kate would continue to have a difficult time with Rufus being gay—she was downright hard on him about it. A part of her was afraid for him, believing his orientation would make his life more difficult, that he would be marginalized, and that AIDS would put him at risk (this was the late eighties). But she was also a little old-fashioned, never able to shake some sort of religious or societal rigidity. She was wild, but she was wild within bounds. As Rufus has pointed out, sometimes liberals and artists are open-minded about other people's sexuality, but when it comes to their own child, they find difference hard to accept. It was all even more inexplicable because Kate herself was bisexual, though she hid it.

With Pat and Rufus gone, she sold the house, and she and I moved into a bright, roomy apartment on Sherbrooke Street a few blocks away. Our old place was filled with a lot of crap, and by the end of the move, I remember we were just emptying stuff from drawers and the tops of dressers into plastic bags. (I seem to have carried the same bits and pieces around for the last twenty years: guitar picks, matches, elastics, coin rollers, rocks from beach trips, miniature playing cards.) Mom did the whole move in her old Ford Taurus that kept on running even after the odometer stopped at two hundred thousand kilometers. I remember one trip where she tied a giant cactus to the roof, steadying it with one hand while steering with the other.

Thinking back, it was probably a hard time for her. A relationship, dismantled. A big house, dismantled. That house had been a testament to Kate's success as an artist—she had bought it with an advance from Warner Bros. Records. On top of that, Rufus, her eldest and favorite child, had left the nest. Or rather, she had pushed him out, for his own good, as she thought.

Which left her with me. Since I had been old enough to understand the words, she had told me how hardheaded I was. She didn't like this quality in me, and I didn't much like it, either, but it's difficult to change that sort of thing. She liked to tell a story from back when I was a toddler. It was Easter, and we were having a little egg hunt inside the house. As a strategy to keep Rufus from finding and hoarding all the eggs, my mom and my grandmother tried to steer me to some of the hiding spots, basically by telling me flat out where they were. *Martha, can you bring me my glasses in the flowerpot over there?* Or, *What's behind that book on the table, Martha?*

Instead of picking up on their hints, I continued my own futile search of the house as Rufus found one colored egg after the next. I'd slide up to where he'd just snatched another egg only to find a pile of nothing. I can't even begin to tell you how many things were wrong with this tactic, and my mom, I think, was always worried that this crappy strategic sense would stay with me my whole life.

Along with the hard head, she also told me I had a chip on my shoulder. For the longest time, I had no idea what she meant, and I would crane my neck to try to spot the chip. But, alongside adoring him, I did have a chip on my shoulder about my brother and accused my mother of loving him more than me. Maybe she did. Kate's song "First Born" is not specifically about Rufus, more about the phenomenon of firstborn sons, but it drove me crazy. (It was made much worse by Rufus's insistence that the song was, in fact, about him.)

That first born son is always the one
The first to be called and the last to come
He's his mother's favorite, grandmother's too
He'll break their hearts and he'll break yours too

Sending Rufus away actually turned out to be a good move. The structure and support of the Millbrook School instilled a great work ethic in him, along with even more confidence and a sense of accomplishment. I guess you get what you pay for. Though he only squeaked by academically, he starred in the school musicals and plays and was really appreciated for that.

As for me, well, I was twelve when Rufus left, and the teenage shit would soon hit the fan. Whether Mom loved him more or not, he was an attention seeker and I had always been in his shadow. Now he was gone and I was ready to be noticed. My mom handled that evolution as she handled most things: with grace and just the faintest disregard. And occasionally, when I really pissed her off—that chip on my shoulder causing me to pick a fight—with fireworks. In other words, I maybe should have gone to Millbrook, too, but her intervention with Rufus was a onetime thing. Kate was not a helicopter mom. She was aware of her kids' rebellions, and now and then concerned about them, but in general she wasn't overly bothered.

After we moved, I transferred from French school to a prim English Protestant girls' school called the Study, which taught its pupils exclusively in English because of a loophole in Quebec's language law. If Rufus got to go to a fancy private school, maybe I should go to one, too. Now I was a real member of the minority Anglo-Montreal population, a skittish group with a false sense of entitlement. I carried around the hymnbook they gave me and sang the verses of "All Things Bright and Beautiful." But whenever we had "free dress" day at school and could abandon the uniform, I showed my true colors. Whereas most girls went for their Sunday best, borrowing their moms' pearl earrings, I wore four or five wide and narrow men's ties simultaneously, along with jeans under a Laura Ashley skirt and a military jacket with patches and epaulets. I took my cues from the silly and extreme fashion of the late eighties, helped along by the endless supply of weird dress-up items we had heaped in dusty baskets around the house: my mom's old clothes from the 1950s and '60s, as well as lots of scarves, belts, hats, and gloves that she had brought home from when she and Pat and Anna were touring the world. Of course, what really inspired me was Pat's look, though I didn't realize it at the time, or even recognize how much I missed him. He had lived with us since I was two, and he was there one day and gone the next.

Thinking back on Kate's decision to send me to the Study, maybe she didn't want me to go away to a boarding school because she liked having me around. Certainly, she was interested in me getting a good education. I even took Latin, for god's sake. I can't say I was a good student, though. Recently, I found some old report cards from back then and I will certainly not be sharing them with my kids.

I have vivid memories of life with Mom in our apartment on Sherbrooke, but one story really sticks out. It was mid-December and Kate was getting ready to throw her annual Christmas party. I was already in bed. Rufus was home from Millbrook, asleep in Kate's bedroom since she was making baked beans, which meant she had to spend the night in the little single bed in the maid's room off the galley kitchen so she could check on them every few hours. She'd left the light on in the kitchen. Tucked into one corner of that room was the small black marble table where she and I often sat for dinner or over coffee in the morning. (It was the table, and the feelings, described in her song "I Eat Dinner": *I eat dinner at the kitchen table with my daughter who is thirteen / We eat leftovers and mashed potatoes / No more candlelight, no more romance, no more small talk when the plate is clean.*)

Sometime in the night, Kate woke to see a figure in the doorway, blocking the light. She could smell alcohol and, at first, she thought it was a friend of hers who had just returned from a trip to Africa. Kate sat up in bed and said, "Nancy?" but the woman did not reply. Instead, the stranger came over and sat down next to her. She touched Kate on the forehead and said, "So this is who you really are."

"Who are you? Who are you?" Kate cried. She said later she didn't want to get out of bed to get away from her because she wasn't wearing any underwear.

Then the figure rose up and ran through the hallway and out the front door. Kate followed her and locked it. She thought about calling the police, but she had a good friend in the neighborhood who was bipolar and in the middle of a manic high, hanging out with some pretty weird people. Perhaps it was one of them? She decided to leave the incident be.

But when she woke up in the bright early morning, she could see signs of the intruder all over the apartment. The electronics—the CD player, the VCR, the phones—had been pulled out of the wall. A pair of Rufus's trousers was tossed on the living room couch. A hammer sat on the little kitchen table near where she had been sleeping, along with a pair of winter gloves that had something on their fingers. Something like mud mixed with the street salt used to melt ice and snow. Then Kate looked down the hall to the front door and saw brown smeared everywhere. When she opened the door, she found a pile of human feces next to the charming old elevator. The intruder had taken a shit in the corridor and had wiped it on the walls.

At that point, Kate called the police. Rufus and I woke up to find our mother explaining the situation to two officers. A sucker for a good story, she couldn't entirely keep a straight face as she recounted the strange, almost comic, sequence of events. I'm sure she felt some fear; fame had brought Kate her share of stalkers. Before the stranger had come to sit on Kate's bed, she had searched for her in the rooms where her children slept. The hammer suggested some potential horror. But I guess Kate's sense that she had dodged something dangerous made her giddy.

Of course, the shit lady was the topic of the night at the Christmas party. Jokes were made about leaving out a roll of toilet paper for the next time she came. In the mundane train of life, such tales keep everyone going. For years, this would be one of Kate's favorite stories to tell; the shit lady became almost like an old friend.

Around that time, my mom and Anna started working on the new music for *Heartbeats Accelerating*, their first album in eight years. Figuring that I was old enough to be left alone, Kate would work late into the night. I started acting out, though I wasn't doing anything all that dramatic. One night, when she was out on a rare date with a new boyfriend, I had my first taste of cheap wine with my best friend from my old French school. Her sister had bought us a bottle of Baby Duck, and I got plastered. When my mother got home, she found me on the bathroom floor, and she held back my hair and wiped my forehead as I threw up. This marked the beginning of my teenage years, with all their sadness and frustration—years that would color my life for a long time.

Another night, Kate and Anna were trying to come to an agreement about whether a song should be on the record. We'd all had a few drinks—my mom didn't actively encourage her kids to drink in her presence, but it wasn't unallowed—and Kate asked me what I thought. When I told her, Anna looked baffled and also a little pissed off. She said it was ridiculous to consider the opinion of a fourteen-year-old girl. When Anna mocked me, I lost control. My aunt is very small, and I'm not, and my mom had to pull me off her.

I couldn't believe what I had just done, but I was glad, too. It had wiped the smile off Anna's face, and even made her cry. It was the first time I'd ever hit an adult, but not the last—aggression I also directed at my own mother. Had this explosion happened because Pat and Rufus were both gone and I was on my own so much? Was it a reaction to my mother's own aggressiveness? She had hit me a few times and could grab or pinch when she was angry. I don't really know.

As Kate and Anna got deeper into their recording, my parents decided that I would go live with my dad in New York for my freshman year of high school. Not so much because I wasn't getting along with Mom, they said, but more because Loudon wanted to try parenting me. Also, Kate and Anna would be away a lot, touring to promote their new record. I was excited but nervous, too; my dad and I had never lived together. Later, he would call that year a disaster. I would call it being a fourteen-year-old girl.

Two

My dad's work comes first. Nothing else matters to him as much—not his partners, not his children. I knew this back then, and I know it now. The year I spent with Loudon involved lots of fights and lots of silences. I learned to lie, and I imagined my dad lied, too.

We lived in an apartment on Twenty-First Street, and I attended Friends Seminary school five blocks south, on Sixteenth at Third. In contrast to my all-girls school in Montreal, Friends Seminary was coed, and more liberal and artsy than I was used to. I convinced myself it was also attendance optional. Like any proper fourteen-year-old, I hated myself. And why not? I was out of my league with these Manhattan kids. I couldn't even spell the word *Manhattan*. Despite being a little less mature than some of my classmates, I quickly learned the ropes. Not with sex—I had no confidence in that department and was a little bit of a prude—but I was soon hanging out with the older kids. I think I was entertaining to them. I started school an angry kid and came out a year later a street-smart teenager.

My new best friend was a girl named Marissa. She was a year older than me and she was both very beautiful and stunningly miserable. Under her influence, I gave up clownish outfits in favor of whatever Marissa wore. Long Indian skirts that hugged her small waist and hourglass hips and turtlenecks that fit tight to her beautiful large breasts. Not quite as effective on me, or so I felt.

Both of us, for different reasons, had little parental supervision. Her father was absorbed by the demands of his new, younger family and his work as a top psychiatrist, and her mother was in Paris. My own father was clueless about how to set boundaries, and my mother was crossing her fingers that we would manage as she and Anna began to tour again. On the one hand, my dad made me do the dishes, since, as he pointed out, he paid for the food, and he also yelled at me to do my homework. On the other hand, he would let me stay out late because he was gone himself. He really had no idea what he was doing. No doubt he had girlfriends he wanted to see, but I think he also stayed out sometimes to get away from me.

As a kid, I listened a lot to my dad's music, trying to find him. To get to know him. I was a big fan of his songs, and often when I was alone, I would play his records on repeat. I had learned to do this because my mother did it, too. She had all his records and had been the one to first play them for me. She was very moved by some of his songs, and by his voice, and I felt proud of him, too. I would bend my ear searching for mentions of me in the lyrics, along with references to my mother and brother. His songs felt like proof that I existed. That I was here. That I was real. That I had been born. It felt sometimes as if I were singing them, as if they were my story, too. But they were not my story, and there were a few times I was deeply disappointed and hurt by his songwriting.

My dad wrote a couple of songs about the year the two of us spent together. One of them, "Hitting You," starts with lyrics about how he once hit me in the back seat of the car when Rufus and I were little. Then it moves on to how he wants to hit me again but stops himself:

> *Long ago I hit you*
> *We were in the car, you were crazy in the back seat*
> *It had gone too far*
> *And I pulled the auto over and hit you with all my might*
> *I knew right away it was too hard and I'd never make*
>   *it right....*
> *These days things are awful between me and you*
> *All we do is argue like two people who are through*
> *I blame you, your school, your mother, and MTV*
> *Last night I almost hit you*
> *That blame belongs to me*

(The other song is called "I'd Rather Be Lonely," and I'll tell you more about it a little later. That one hurt more.)

The year of discontent my forty-four-year-old father spent with his fourteen-year-old daughter was one he hoped to forget but that I still remember fondly. I kept my dad from what he really wanted to be doing, which was music and being by himself, which tortured him as much as anything I got up to. But I had fun smoking pot, riding the subway at night, and meeting all these different, mostly rich, sometimes famous kids (Susan Sarandon dropped her children off at the seminary every morning) who lived in lofts in SoHo or big apartments on the Upper East Side. I had my first aching and, of course, unrequited crush that year, on a senior who lived in a brownstone in Brooklyn Heights. He was tall and good-looking and he was madly in love with Marissa. Deep down, I understood why. I was in love with her, too.

Having never spent so much time together, my dad and I remained uncomfortable and shy with each other. But even though I was a shit—which at that age was my job—I also really liked being around him and my sister, Lucy, and her mom, Suzzy, and that whole side of my extended family. Suzzy and Lucy lived in the West Village, and I would go over for dinner sometimes or for a girls' night when Dad was away. My late grandfather's much younger second wife, Martha Fay, still lived in the apartment where most of my childhood New York City visits were spent. His first wife, my maternal grandmother, was Martha Taylor Wainwright, and one of Loudon's two sisters was named Martha, too, though she was always called Aunt Teddy. (I know it's crazy—four Marthas in one family!) The apartment, which she shared with her daughter, Anna—my aunt, though she is ten years younger than me—was filled with books and pictures; Martha Fay is an incredible person and a great cook, who took great care of me. Her place was a home away from home, and remained that way for many years.

Suzzy was a singer, too, and still is, one-third of the Roches, a New York–based folk act that her big sisters, Maggie and

Terre Roche, had started in the 1970s, but that really took off when Suzzy joined a little later. You think it would be awkward between us, because Loudon had left my mother for Suzzy, or at least that's how my mom framed it. (I could ask Suzzy, but I wouldn't want to put her on the spot. I do remember as a kid finding naked pictures of her, and pictures of her sitting on my mom's couch in my parents' house in Woodstock. Putting two and two together is a part of growing up.) Even though Lucy was six years younger than me, we had become close over the years of summer visits, and it had always been a little sad to leave each other at the end of a vacation, especially for Lucy, who was an only child and liked having siblings around.

Also that year, I became more like my father, as if the DNA in me that came from him started to wake up, almost like a switch got turned on. Just by being around him and that side of my family, I felt like I had added facets to my life and my personality. It's hard to explain, like I grew new feathers or spots. I can only imagine how much more I would be like him if we'd had a little more time together—a little more time to learn how to be together. It maybe would have made things easier between us, and for me, in the long run.

Rufus and I had always been more influenced by Kate than my dad. When my brother and I were young and went to visit Loudon on Shelter Island (or as Lucy calls it, Tension Island— because my dad is tense in many ways), he'd try to impose his way of doing things on us. He wanted us to have summer jobs, to make our own money with paper routes and such, whereas Kate didn't necessarily believe in pushing kids in that way. She wanted us to do well in school, learn to play instruments, and eventually write songs or lose ourselves in books and art or whatever. My father is disciplined; he practices and exercises according to a daily routine. It keeps him sane. He is also punctual, either right on time or a bit early, whereas I'm always late.

I disappointed my father more than once being late, making him wait at a restaurant for fifteen minutes, half an hour, or more. Rufus has a great song about Loudon called "Dinner at Eight." If I had written the song, it would be called "Dinner at Fucking 8:45" and it would have told the story of an older man waiting impatiently for his flaky daughter to show up for a strained dinner date. Why did I do that so often to the both of us? Why would I leave Brooklyn at 7:45, seventeen subway stops away from his apartment, already guilty because I knew it would take an hour for me to get there and that Loudon would be angry? I was most likely stoned and he most likely knew it. (Rufus also has a song called "Martha" that laments the fact that I never call him back. So you can see the reputation I have in my family.)

Maybe I tortured my dad (and sometimes still do) because I was mad at him. Mad at him for almost denying my existence and for being so impatient with me as a teenager. For being so good at what he does and for committing his life to his art without compromise. That must be it. I'm a little jealous—of his freedom, his confidence, and his more disciplined approach to his career.

Some good things came out of that year I spent with my dad.

A math teacher helped me identify my life path. I was good at math and, like most of my teachers, she was disappointed that I had lots of potential but not much of a work ethic. One day she got so frustrated, she blurted out, "What do you want to do all your life—sing and dance?" I don't think I responded, but then and there, I quit worrying about what I was going to be or do when I grew up. "Sing and dance"—it had a ring to it. I had been onstage singing and dancing for years, but it had never occurred to me that I could do it for a living. Because my parents did it, I didn't see it as glamorous, and had thought I would do something else. But it was sure easier than calculus.

If you're an artist, your kids are bound to end up artists, too. To put it another way, once you're in the circus, it's hard to get out.

Three

AFTER MY YEAR IN NEW YORK, my mom and I were happy to be reunited; we had missed each other. We moved to Outremont, a slightly hipper neighborhood. I was hipper, too, and so was Kate. I also had to change schools, because I had failed the academic year in New York, having spent a little bit too much time in Washington Square Park, hanging out and smoking dope.

College Rachel's mix of students was much different than the crowd at my first all-girls school: Haitian girls who came from Montreal-Nord, a working-class neighborhood on the edge of the island, a lot of girls from the Portuguese community, and then girls like me, who couldn't get in anywhere else. The classes were conducted in French, which kicked my ass since I hadn't had to function in French since fifth grade. Under the influence of my new girlfriends, I quickly became a separatist and wore lots of eyeliner, gazing out at the world from behind a plume of cigarette smoke as we gathered over beers after school in the nearby pool halls, leaning over the tables in our hiked-up uniforms.

College Rachel had an unexpectedly good theater department, the productions so strong that professional actors would often perform alongside us. When we put on Michel Tremblay's *Les Belles-soeurs*, he came to see it. Tremblay is Quebec's most famous playwright, living or dead, and his plays are staged around the world. This one is a fast-paced, joual-laced social commentary on the grip of Catholicism in Quebec in the sixties, as seen through the lives of several working-class women in the Plateau-Mont-Royal in Montreal—a far cry from Manhattan's stoner Quakers. We also did Molière's *Le malade imaginaire* and Ionesco's *Rhinoceros*. I had had plenty of onstage experience, but it was in the context of singing with my parents—often their songs and sometimes songs about me—always being overly earnest and true. But in theater I could be somebody else, and I think that is what appealed to me the most. My face, my body, and my voice can be quite chameleon-like, and for a fifteen- and sixteen-year-old, I was a convincing actor. Also, I identified with the characters, their anger, loneliness, and stupidity—I felt those, too. Performing in these plays, under the direction of a French-from-France director (whose name I can't remember), pushed me toward the idea of going to acting school. I figured becoming an actor might set me apart from the rest of my family and put me on a path where I wouldn't risk having to become an accountant, or whatever it is people like to say is the opposite of a musician. (Actually, my father had gone to acting school and, these days, surviving in the music business demands a fair bit of accounting. The apple does not fall far from the guitar.)

The country's best school, the National Theatre School of Canada, was just up the street from College Rachel, so in my last year of CEGEP (Quebec's equivalent of precollege), I prepared a monologue from *Antigone* and auditioned. Of course, they rejected me (that's often a part of my story). Concordia, the less famous English-speaking university in Montreal, also had a theater program, so I decided to try there, preparing something from the John Ford Noonan play *All She Cares About Is the Yankees*. That play was my father's recommendation and maybe I was trying to get closer to him by going to acting school. I was terribly hungover when I did my audition, but they accepted me. Unfortunately, I got it in my head that because this worked in my favor the one time, it would continue to work in my favor.

Along with the girls from College Rachel, I hung out with kids from the neighborhood who were into music and poetry and philosophy and smoking. I came off as mature for my age and had an edge because I had lived in New York. One of the kids, Sara, was particularly confident and took it upon herself to mount and direct the musical *Hair*, which was not an easy task. Basically, anyone in the neighborhood who wanted to get involved could, but most of the participants were pulled from Sara's own school, known to be a bit of a slacker institution with lots of Anglos. Perfect for the cast of *Hair*. I played all the parts no one else wanted and sang all the impossible songs— remember "Manchester England, England"?

This is how I met my best friend to this day, Ariel. We were opposites who somehow fit like hand and glove. As teenagers, our relationship was complex. I envied her and was also in love with her. She was, and still is, very beautiful, and at the time that is what I envied most. Many of my best girlfriends were more sexually precocious than I was and very beautiful. I don't know why that was a pattern, but it definitely made me into more of a joker, a loudmouth, and a slightly tragic character—feeding my appetite for attention, drugs and alcohol, fun and love.

I spent a lot of time at Ariel's house. Her parents, educators not artists, were together, unlike mine, and had created a very loving home. I grew attached to them (I was always on the hunt for a father figure), along with Ariel. In contrast, she appreciated my mother's sometimes loose rules and the bohemian aspect of my home. But we spent more time at her place because my mom was so intense. We tended to hang out and play house in my apartment when Kate wasn't around.

Ariel and I had boyfriends, but we were also kind of girl-friends. Everybody in our circle knew, but it wasn't really talked about and seemed like the most natural thing. Teenagers weren't as vocal about their gender and sexual identity then as they are today, though everybody was doing all the same things they do now (I presume). Kate didn't seem to care, or maybe she was happier that I was experimenting sexually with a girl rather than a boy, though it seemed like she was applying somewhat of a double standard given the way she had reacted to Rufus. I felt lucky that Ariel was the object of my desire, and that I was hers. Simply put, it was love.

Kate was sad that I liked spending so much time with Ariel and her parents, but I always returned home to her. I needed my mom. She wanted me to be the best I could be, but I have never had her drive and sheer intelligence. Or I felt undermined in those regards because I was very emotionally vulnerable. I was often intimidated by the people around me, and didn't know how to shape myself into something great—something I so desperately wanted to be.

After I graduated, I went on to theater school, which, to be honest, I didn't take that seriously, because how can anyone really? In first year, I didn't even get to act. Our job, as new students, was to launder the costumes of the students in higher grades who were the ones who actually got to perform. The company was a *whole*, our instructors kept telling us, urging us to strip ourselves of whatever affectations or attitudes we might be using as crutches. They wanted a blank slate. I may have been insecure, but blank slates are hard for me.

By then, Rufus had graduated from Millbrook and moved back home to Montreal. I watched with interest, and some skepticism, as he began to write songs and build a career, and that became my new school. I started out singing backup for him and soon began writing my own songs, stealing away to my room and putting pen to paper as I strummed out chords on the Sigma guitar my father had given me when I was thirteen, and that I hadn't used all that much to this point. I kept the songwriting a secret. I didn't want anyone to hear me fumbling around. Still, I was starting to harvest, not lose, my affectations and attitudes. No more washing other people's laundry in public. From now on, I concentrated on my own dirty laundry.

I only lasted a year and a half in theater school, once more disappointing my mother.

* * *

Rufus, my mom, and I hadn't lived together since we were all under the same roof with Pat in the big house on the hill in Westmount, and we converged again after each of us had gone through something major. Kate and Anna had released an incredible album and made a formidable return to the world stage. Rufus had survived boarding school—quite well, too—but now he was ready to live his life as a young gay male in ways he hadn't been able to do yet. I had survived a year with my father, which, much as I loved him, was essentially like living in enemy territory.

We all loved Outremont, but our flat was a dump. When we first moved in, we lived out of bags and boxes. We had no fridge, but luckily it soon turned cold, so we were able to store milk and other perishables between the interior and the storm windows. Kate bought some metal camping dishes and she would often make our new favorite meal of soba noodle soup— basically hot water poured over soba noodles, tofu, and watercress, with soy sauce and sesame oil added to taste. I wouldn't necessarily call us survivalists, but the scene definitely appealed to our free-spiritedness. Kate liked anything that reminded her of her own bohemian youth.

Rufus slept in the front parlor, which he painted red, yellow, and dark blue. My mom had the room off the dining room and laid a futon on the floor. I lived in a little room off the kitchen, near the back staircase, which led to the alley and enabled countless midnight escapes and escapades. Not that my mom altogether objected, although I don't know if she fully understood what I was up to. We were all three forging a new adult relationship that was both comforting and confusing, and she wavered over what kind of mother to be. She stayed up late with us listening to music and didn't mind us drinking, but she drew the line at dope, and she pushed us to succeed, at least somewhat, in school. Or pushed me.

Kate was often frustrated with me to the point of being hurtful. She broke some cardinal parenting rules, like talking shit about my dad, but then she would raise him up to an almost godlike position, saying how great a singer he was and that he was underappreciated. She also said it was his own fault because he didn't play the game, disregarding other people's opinions and making self-defeating decisions. (I think she recognized these attitudes of his in me.) She couldn't always control her temper, but I couldn't control mine either. There were scenes. She occasionally told me I was mediocre. I don't think she meant it. At least I hope not. The hardest thing for me to take was when she seemed disappointed in me.

She loved talking about her childhood. Even as a little kid, Kate was wild. She had what they referred to as St. Vitus's dance, which was the Catholic diagnosis for ADHD or something similar. She was always flying around like a Tasmanian devil and getting into trouble. She swung cats by their tails and kicked people in the shins. She was very physical, as well as brainy. Like a lot of kids with ADHD, she had a lot going on in her mind that she was able to turn into something remarkable when she found an outlet for it, whether it was singing or playing instruments. Or getting a degree in physics.

She especially liked remembering the tales of her wild, misfit youth and all the parties she and Anna had thrown in their various flats. After she had left home, she had surrounded herself with artists and musicians. I remember a story she told about how she and a bunch of her friends once took acid. They cooked a bunch of spaghetti with food coloring in it, ate it, and then made themselves throw up so they could see the colors. That seemed pretty crazy to me. Was she daring me to be more wild? I don't think so. I think she liked talking to her kids and letting them know who she was and what she had seen.

The three of us would end most days with wine and music. Kate and Rufus were formidable characters and they both made me slightly nervous. My mom wanted me to be more like *them*, but I was more plainspoken, more earnest. Kate disliked my earnestness, and I admit it was boring from the inside, too. Overall, though, that period for me was a musical and cultural education, courtesy of my mom and my brother, both so curious and smart. Rufus was particularly interested in classical music—he attended the conservatory at McGill for a year when he came back to Montreal—but both he and Kate admired any music that was risk-taking and inspired. *Eclectic* was the prerequisite, at least for me. Bahamian slap guitar. Norwegian folk songs. *Le Mystère des Voix Bulgares*. Paco de Lucía. Arvo Pärt. Fleetwood Mac's *Rumours*. Nina Simone. John Cale. Laurie Anderson. Ewan MacColl. Stephen Foster and John McCormack. Lots and lots of Verdi and Puccini; any and all of the classical composers. Blind Willie Johnson. Bessie Smith. Ella Fitzgerald. Miles Davis. Along with Fergus

MacRoy, a pseudonym for Galt MacDermot (who wrote several hit musicals, including *Hair*), and another of my mom's favorites, a trio of San Francisco buskers known as Richard, Cam & Bert, who made a single album whose sound my mom liked. The sound, maybe, of no one listening.

Kate believed that good taste is learned, not innate. When Rufus and I were younger, she let us listen to Casey Kasem's *American Top 40* on pop radio, but in limited doses. She allowed Michael Jackson, Prince, Cyndi Lauper, and Boy George, but Madonna not so much. As kids, Rufus and I both loved *Peter Pan* and *Oliver!*, and Rufus wanted to be Annie in *Annie*, which irked my mother to no end, but the musicals stopped there. Rufus also loved the soundtrack of the film *That's Entertainment!*, especially the parts with Judy Garland and Mickey Rooney, whereas my mother merely tolerated it.

She didn't much like me listening to Joni Mitchell, either, but I imagine she envied her huge success. (I understand. I like Feist, but I don't want her records blasting in my house on repeat.) I don't think my mom was all that pleased by how much I listened to Leonard Cohen. He was already famous, after all, and hardly needed extra support from her daughter.

She did take me to see him in Montreal once, when he was playing at the Théâtre Saint-Denis. It was in 1988, after his *I'm Your Man* album was released. I became obsessed with it, playing the cassette over and over on my small, blue boom box. I think that record all on its own sent me teetering from pained puberty toward young adulthood.

The show was magical and confirmed my desire to be one of

Leonard's backup singers when I grew up. He put them up in front and sang to them. They would respond with their voices, as well as with their movements and eyes, part of a dance between him and them that wasn't just sexual and sensual, but an expression of humans in an animal state. More than anything, it showed me the power and importance of backup singers.

In 1994, when I was eighteen, Kate put together all her savings and bought a triplex on Querbes Avenue in Montreal, the same building I live in now, a warm and fuzzy cage I am extremely fond of. The renovations nearly drove Kate to suicide, or so she said at the time. The work took several years to complete. Eventually Rufus and I moved in, too, at first sharing one of the flats and then each having our own. As ever, Kate gave us a lot of freedom.

I lived on the ground floor with my first real boyfriend, Kate was in the middle, and Rufus was perched on top. Other than the fact that each floor had a piano, the apartments were reflections of their inhabitants. I was always flip-flopping between wanting to be myself and wanting to be more normal, settle down, have children, the whole bit. I tried, but failed, to keep a neat apartment. I loved my boyfriend a lot and we remained together on and off for several years, but he also turned out to have some big problems. Worse, he often made me feel like there was something wrong with me when there wasn't. He was gorgeous and smart, but also unhappy and secretive (another theme in my life with men). Although he loved me back, he couldn't always show it. His withholding fed my insecurities about my attractiveness and set me up for a succession of subsequent rejections that broke my confidence. I don't want to say that everything in this area is determined by men, but when you're a young, mostly heterosexual woman, it's really a big issue. I lost my virginity at seventeen (which I thought was old) with a conga player in a psychedelic blues band. But when I told my mother, she was angry with me. She said, "Now you will know what it is to be under the power of a man." Maybe she had been drinking. Her reaction certainly seemed a little over the top. I'm sure she was just doing her best, but it sometimes felt like she was trying to toughen me up.

Even though the building renovations had practically bankrupted her, my mom still insisted that Rufus and I do what we cared about, so long as we gave it our all. Not once did she push us to work regular jobs. I think she already believed that Rufus could make it someday, and that maybe I could, too, and she wanted to help make that happen.

Rufus and I were already singing together by the time we moved into the triplex on Querbes Avenue. We were a somewhat reluctant duo, two people who needed each other at first and then needed to break apart. Our musical partnership was complicated, even if loving. For one, it wasn't a partnership. Rufus wrote the songs and told me what to sing on them. He was a real older brother. When I was little, I had followed him around like a puppy, and when we started singing together, I did the same thing. He savored the attention—surprise, surprise.

I was also now privy to his social life, to the gay bars he frequented, and to the edgy and sometimes reckless characters who surrounded him. At times, he and I were extremely reckless ourselves. He was popular, smart, funny, mean, driven, and wild, and his friends were intriguing. I was his right-hand man a lot of the time and I was honored to be that. In time, I realized I needed to find my own way, but for now I was learning from the best.

Rufus's songs from this time were about a sexually ambiguous heroin addict he was in love with and the nighttime escapades that were the backdrop of so much of his life. Songs like "Danny Boy," "Beauty Mark," and "Cigarettes and Chocolate Milk," about beautiful people and heartbreak and also the unmatched, indescribable love he had for our mother.

Around 1995, Rufus began a regular Wednesday night gig at a local club called the Sarajevo, a hole-in-the-wall on Clark Street just off Saint-Laurent, a run-down boulevard that was home to dive bars and old-school Jewish delis and machine shops. It had a piano in one corner and hosted live music performances a few nights a week, mostly jazz and world-music trios with funny instruments and sad faces. The club was dark and usually half-empty, run by a Serbo-Croatian husband-and-wife team who had recently escaped the war in Yugoslavia. They served small plates of Yugoslavian food they would prepare upstairs in their apartment to accompany the copious amounts of booze the patrons were throwing back downstairs. Until Rufus started playing there, no one paid much attention to the performers. There weren't all that many gay boys playing flowery pop songs on an acoustic piano back in 1995 in Montreal, Canada. Kate suggested that she and I lean a full-length mirror on its side along the lonely black piano so that everyone in the audience could see Rufus's face. An old show-biz trick, it turns out, but with a face like Rufus's, it really worked. The mirror added an extra layer of intimacy and a sense of outward reflection that fit Rufus perfectly. And now he had a professional reason to spend time looking at himself, something he always loved to do.

We'd been part of the local arts scene for a couple of years at the time, getting onstage at happenings called YAWPs that were held in different loft and basement venues around town. Hosted by an angry, restless poetry teacher, urban cowboy, and cult-leader type named Jake, the YAWPs were a variety show of music, spoken word, theater, and clowning (I'm sure YAWP stands for something, but I never knew what). There was some ska punk and street music around, but not a lot of singer-songwriters, unlike New York—the East Village was crawling with song-writers in the nineties. There were no Jeff Buckleys in Montreal, so not that much competition, but there was serious talent.

Our friend Tom Mennier, a classically trained pianist with clear, raw talent, would play, along with clowns and dancers who would go on to be very successful (Joe De Paul, Catherine Kidd, Heather O'Neill). Lhasa de Sela had shown up in town, and we sang background vocals for a not-so-great reggae band. I spent a few nights in her basement apartment, drinking tea and listening to her stories, her words and laughter as captivating as her music. She had not yet met the Montreal musicians who would collaborate with her on her incredible first record, but it was obvious she was special. The scene was all very underground and a bit freakish—lots of crazy piercings and tattoos, anarchist-vegan café life and zine publications.

Rufus already had *star* written all over him. I, on the other hand, did not, but I will say that whenever I opened my mouth to sing, people listened. Eventually Rufus let me sing a couple of my own songs during his show at the Sarajevo—my mom must have insisted. At moments like these, Kate was in artist-mom heaven. She was also happy with the size of the crowds at the Sarajevo—young, old, gay, straight, though never *too* straight—but mostly she was happy to see all the love directed at Rufus.

She went all out in her support. Sometimes she even volunteered to collect the cover charge from incoming patrons. Perched on a stool by the door, like a gypsy tarot card reader in her long skirt, headscarf, and loud bangles on both wrists, with a black money box resting on her lap, she looked and acted like she ran the place. The smoky ambience, the cheap Moroccan-chic vibe, the aura of subterranean illegality, the characters who matched my mom's bohemian spirit—she loved the whole scene. (That's another thing we had in common: an attraction to and tolerance for nutty people.) The overflowing crowds on Wednesday nights must have reminded her of the clubs and coffee shops she'd played when she was starting out.

Today, when I picture my mom, up swirls a composite of her on that stool and of all the things and all the people she ever was and ever wanted to be—a beatnik poet, an Egyptian queen, a devoted nun, an Irish Republican, a Bolshevik or a czar, a stargazer, a scientist, a pilgrim walking the Compostela trail, or a nineteenth-century adventurer riding into the desert dusk on a camel's hump.

One day, needing to make some money, I asked the Sarajevo's owners if I could do some bartending and waiting on tables, and they said yes. I got right into the social aspects of tending bar. One drink for you, one for me! As you can imagine, my employment didn't last long, but I played the role of the singing waitress for a solid two months before I put down my dishrag and picked up a guitar for good. My fantasy was that I'd be like Sophia Loren in an Italian rural bar, abused and battered by her customers, who, in retaliation, breaks into a song that breaks their hearts and brings everyone to tears. But that never happened. I'm less Sophia Loren and more Anna Magnani.

The truth is, after watching Rufus get all the attention every week, I was envious. Growing up, I never played the piano—how could I with my brother wailing away on it day and night? The guitar is a more private instrument, better for me, but I didn't really start to play until I was seventeen. My mom showed me a few chords, and I proceeded to learn a few Elvis tunes and some country songs. Country music was a big influence on me in my late teens. When I was in CEGEP, a friend and I hosted a little country music radio show, and I liked singing in that style. I recently reconnected with that friend and he reminded me that he would do all the work, collecting and bringing in records and talking about the musicians, and I would just wax poetic about how it all made me feel. It's amazing how little we change.

The plaintive, lonely country sound and sad stories appealed to me, and from that style, my first couple of songs were born. Of course, they were about my family. The very first was called "Question of Etiquette," or "The Lexie Song." (Many of my early songs had two titles. I just couldn't commit. It's not good to have two titles: it's bad for collecting publishing and it's confusing. This was the first of many mistakes I'd make in the music business.) It was about the birth of my brand-new half sister, Lexie, born in 1994 to my father and Ritamarie Kelly, a woman he had dated for a few years. I wanted to let that little baby know, sooner rather than later, the lay of the dysfunctional family land.

I had met Ritamarie on a trip to the West Coast with my dad when I was thirteen. We went to see her do her one-woman show in LA. She did impressions, including one of Linda Ronstadt singing Mexican songs in a big sombrero. I thought she was hilarious. (We also went bowling with Lucinda Williams on that trip. Given my dad's past, I assumed they were sleeping together, but who knows. He's a bit of a slut, which I've always found somewhat impressive.) But back to the song, which I still find pleasing, especially in the way it jauntily assures the infant not to be frightened of the family unit. Though perhaps a warning would have been more useful:

> *Met you for the first time late last week*
> *You came to dinner, it could have been bleak*
> *But I held back, held myself on track*
> *Question of etiquette or maybe just regret....*
> *I've got a brother you might want to meet*

He can be yours, it's really kind of neat
Oh I hope my mother doesn't pull a fit, she always thinks
  this stuff is bullshit
There'll be Christmas and holidays, weddings and funerals....
Question of etiquette or maybe just regret...oh baby, there's
  no regret

It was the beginning of my own confessional style of song-writing, autobiographical and gory in all its details. It's both unsurprising and a little disappointing that my first song can be added to a long list of songs that members of my family have written "to" or "about" one another. Somehow, when holding an instrument, our WASPy guard dissolves and we vomit out our feelings—so long as they rhyme. This, of course, can be a bad idea, but it's something I do, over and over again. From all appearances, it seems that I've chosen the stage, and the parameters of a song, as a natural place to communicate emotions I can't always say aloud in the course of a normal conversation. The phrase "question of etiquette" is somewhat meaningless, which is why I kind of like it. In a lot of my songs there are lines or phrases that are poetic or simply evocative of something, rather than being exact. I feel they better express what I mean.

When Rufus let me sing this one, and a couple of my others, during his set and the people in the audience liked them, I was energized and motivated. Still, it wasn't enough to propel me into full-on songwriting. That takes dedication and drive, and I just wasn't there yet.

I kept on singing backup for Rufus, live (and later, on his first two records), attempting to emulate Leonard Cohen's backup singers while dueting on songs such as "Sally Ann" and "In My Arms," for example. I was always trying to draw attention to myself, and that was the last thing Rufus wanted. A couple of factors finally pushed me to dedicate myself to my own music. First, Rufus landed a big record deal with DreamWorks, the second person to be signed by the new company after George Michael, and the first artist that cochair Lenny Waronker signed to the new label. (Lenny had signed up Kate and Anna's debut album in his old job at Warners; my dad had passed Rufus's demo tape to the musician, composer, and arranger Van Dyke Parks, who had passed it on to Lenny.) I won't ever forget my mom, stunned and amazed, looking over Rufus's fifty-page contract in his apartment at Querbes, surrounded by his loud paintings. It was a good deal, maybe one of the last good ones. The record industry hadn't fallen apart yet, and music executives were still throwing a lot of money around.

The second thing: when that contract came through, Rufus decided to move to LA. He was getting famous and I was faltering (flailing). He needed to cut the fat and I needed to get out of his shadow. But he never got rid of me fully, and I never got out of his shadow. We always needed each other. I needed him more than he needed me, yet I served a purpose. I was his biggest fan. I still am.

But when he left, I knew I needed to get out of Montreal, too.

Four

Around that time, I met the person who would not only get me out of the house, but out onto the road, too. Dan Bern was and still is a singer-songwriter. You couldn't pay him to stop writing songs. He'll probably write songs from his grave.

I was twenty-one, on the outs with my longtime boyfriend, or it might have just been the sex, but I fell deeply and painfully in love with Dan, which would turn out to be the beginning of a habit. Cringey, yes, absolutely, but a dynamic that certainly fueled my songwriting and fed into a period of self-pity and uncertainty that was hard to shake.

It was 1997, and I'd traveled down to the Philadelphia Folk Festival to sing with Kate and Anna. When we arrived, the festival was abuzz with talk about a young songwriter some people were calling the new Bob Dylan (such a drag). Dan had a super nasally voice, was Jewish, came from the Midwest, and wrote about politics and the news of the day. He tried to shake off the comparison at the same time as taking it to new heights. But more than his Dylan-esque attitude, it was his screwball sex appeal and slightly shocking lyrics that really got the crowd going.

To understand why, it's important to remember that the Philly Folk Fest is filled with repressed folksy types in sun hats and awful sandals, the women often in tank tops displaying giant breasts—*folk tits*, as a friend referred to them—that you could see clearly from the stage. Which is why when Dan began talking about his "big balls," it got the crowd's ear and made all the females laugh nervously, including me. ("I got big old balls, big as the swing on Tiger Woods...") I blush when I think back on this (even now, I'm a bit of a prude), but I was very forward toward Dan. Having drunk a few beers, I snuck inside his dressing room after watching his set and left a note in his guitar case. I can't remember exactly what the note said, but it did mention his big balls, and also what a curious young woman I was. Actually, I do remember what it said, but I'm trying to learn to hold back.

That night when the festival ended, I boarded the shuttle bus back to the motel where the musicians were all staying. The new Dylan got on the bus a few seconds later, and it became clear that he had read my note. Back at the hotel, my mom and aunt invited him along with a few others to their room for a nightcap, and we all played songs and talked about our lives. I found him very intriguing and charming. When I retired for the night, I left my motel room door unlocked, and not that long afterward he found me. (Recounting this story now, I can't help wondering whether he could just as easily have spent the night with Kate. I think my mom and I were thinking the same thing when it came to Dan, but she could tell I liked him and approved. It's probably just a false memory, but I wanted so much to be like her or for her to like me.)

Since Dan was staying on, I also remained at the festival after my mom left. Suzzy Roche was playing there, too, and once Mom was gone, I hung out with Suzzy, who was always supportive of me and my music and was kind enough to let me play a couple of songs during her set. It was one of my first times singing my own stuff in front of a lot of people. I loved Suzzy, which upset my mother. The Suzzy thing was always hard for her, and I was torn, but I looked up to Suzzy. She and my father still adored each other and remained the closest of friends. Of all his exceptional girlfriends, she was the most important to him. He asked her to marry him twice, but she never wanted to. She valued her independence.

When Dan moved on, I went with him, and for the next couple of weeks, we bummed around, traveling from gig to gig. I felt like a character in a road movie. He was doing well for himself, and I hoped this was the beginning of an amazing romantic and musical partnership. I ignored a few warning signs. A few days into our trip, for example, Dan admitted to me that he had lied about his age when we were all talking in Kate's motel room. He wasn't thirty-two, as he had claimed, but thirty-eight.

Dan must have already realized that a relationship with the highly emotional twenty-one-year-old girl he had gotten himself involved with was not a viable thing. I'd like to think that Dan was attracted to me, and to my music, but I don't know if that's true and I never will. Most, if not all, of the men I've been involved with are drawn to my family. I'm not saying my family is the only reason they like me, but it certainly piques their interest.

In the meantime, though, Dan and I drove around the East Coast, smoking a lot of pot. We stared into each other's eyes for hours. We made love outside under the sky and drank wine on the banks of rivers or perched on the hood of his car. We sang together. We laughed a lot. When you think about it, I had no chance. I didn't go back to school in Montreal, devoting myself to following my troubadour around on his tours.

On a few occasions, other girls showed up, approaching Dan during sound checks as if they belonged there, and by the way, who was I? Their faces would fall once they realized I was staying in Dan's Winnebago. He kept insisting I was his number one. Can you believe men actually say that to women? "Don't worry, baby. You're my number one."

Thus began a spiral downward that felt like it lasted forever, but could probably also be seen as a necessary rite of passage. At least I got some good songs out of it, including "Year of the Dragon," a song I wrote after meeting Dan, and the first song I ever recorded for an album, in this case, *The McGarrigle Hour*. (Yes, it features only close relations, the free-spirited circus troupe that was my family.)

Dan, his band, and I spent most of the next year traveling around the United States. We stopped for a long time in Boulder, Colorado, where he made a record that includes several songs about me. I sing on it, too. The title track is "Smartie Mine." *Smartie*—that's what Dan used to call me.

His lyrics were overt and sexual, which I appreciated. He had a strong influence on me musically, though our approach to songwriting is very different. Dan writes maybe five songs a week, whereas I write maybe five songs in a good year. We dueted on a song I wrote called "Babylove" that's really kind of beautiful but also awkward and exposed—exactly the way I was. When Dan exposed himself in a song, the impact was powerful and compelling. When I exposed myself, the audience required some strength to be able to withstand it. Or at least that's what I thought.

During all this time, Rufus was in LA, making his record. I would go out there, sometimes just to see him and sometimes to sing backup. On my first trip, when Rufus picked me up at the airport, he told me we had an event to go to that night and took me straight to Fred Segal, where I bought a Betsey Johnson dress. Because the distances are so rangy in LA, we didn't have time to swing by the Oakwood apartments, where he was staying, so I pulled the dress on in the car. (We also dropped by a CVS to buy me some deodorant, which I thought would be a good idea to wear that night. Something I rarely did, and still don't.)

Then we were off to a dinner at the Ivy restaurant with Lenny Waronker, and by 6 a.m. the next morning Rufus and I were at Stephen Stills's house, doing blow. What happened in between is a bit blurry, but that night launched both my love affair with, and slight disdain for, Los Angeles.

I do remember that the dinner at the Ivy was amazing. The

place may have fallen out of favor since then, but it was very exciting at the time to be drinking whiskey sours and spotting stars behind giant palm leaves and lounging on wicker furniture under art deco archways. Rufus had been wined and dined a lot, so he was more used to it. Lenny was charming, funny, and nice, and Rufus was very comfortable around him. In our family, Lenny was golden, one of the few people in the top echelons of the music industry who fully embraced us.

Later that night, we met up with some of my brother's new friends, including Chris Stills, Stephen Stills's son. Rufus had become part of a "sons of" group, including Chris, Adam Cohen (Leonard's son), Richard and Linda Thompson's son, Teddy, and Sean Lennon. These rock sons were coming of age in Los Angeles, New York, and London, and there were pretty girls and labels chasing them, lots of parties to go to, and lots of songs to sing. It was easy to tell that they each wanted to usurp their father; it was fun to watch but also hard to watch. Though Rufus was a member in good standing, he was confident in a way a lot of them were not, neither bothered nor deterred by the so-called shadow of his parents. He had been coddled by our mother and mostly neglected by our father, and neither of them had careers that intimidated him. My parents are both impressive artists, but not full-blown stars, which left Rufus with less family baggage to deal with.

I thought all these men were kind of dreamy, but the person I felt for the most was Chris Stills. Male beauty is always irresistible to me, and he's one of the most beautiful men in the world (you're welcome, Chris). Also, the night we met, he opened up to me, telling me personal and sad things about his upbringing, which of course made me adore him even more and want to take care of him. We had some late-night, clumsy version of sex—the Betsey Johnson dress was off for a while—but that wasn't the important part.

His dad's gold records were up on the walls of their house in the Hollywood Hills, and people were doing a lot of coke, and it was both stupid and fun at the same time. In the morning, when Stephen Stills's children from a later marriage came downstairs for cereal, it didn't feel right to keep doing lines in the now sunny kitchen, so we put our sunglasses on and stumbled out of the mansion like so many people had done before us.

Back at the Oakwoods, Rufus and I ran into a neighbor, William H. Macy, who had just done *Fargo*, which creeped me out a bit given that here we were in a carpeted eighties kitsch hallway that could have been straight out of the movie. After that, we crawled into the apartment, pulled the blinds, and slept.

Funnily enough, Rufus and I had stayed in a short-term rental at one of the Oakwood buildings back in 1985, when Mom and Pat had brought us to LA on a family trip. There are a few Oakwoods in LA, but the one we stayed in then was near Universal Studios. We visited Disneyland during that trip, and then ended up moving over to the Chateau Marmont for some reason, maybe because it was Grammy week and we naturally gravitated, or rose, to the stars. You can just imagine the scene. Cyndi Lauper, Tina Turner, and Eurythmics were all staying or hanging at the Marmont. I watched one of my idols, Annie Lennox, check in, and we ran into Cyndi Lauper, another of my idols, later that evening, in the hot tub. I remember she was very nervous, biting her nails and pulling at her hair, and she wore no makeup and a beige bathing suit that made her look naked. Only in LA.

Rufus was recording at Ocean Way studios in Hollywood, a fabled place. The Rolling Stones were working in the next studio over. The Stones recorded at night, and once, after we'd downed a bunch of margaritas at El Chavo restaurant, a favorite of ours on Sunset Boulevard, we went back to the studio to see if we could catch a glimpse of them...or maybe offer up guest vocals by brother-and-sister Canadian folk singers. Why not?

We stumbled up to the door, clearly drunk, claiming that Rufus had forgotten his wallet inside. Security didn't buy it and escorted us off the premises. So we didn't end up rubbing shoulders with Mick or Keith that night (although we did spot Mick in the hall eating a banana one time).

Rufus's producer was Jon Brion, who had just come off working with Fiona Apple. My brother and Jon butted heads a lot. Rufus knew what he wanted, Jon sometimes wanted something else, and by halfway through the project, Jon and Rufus weren't speaking. Rufus felt like Jon couldn't bear him having input. At one point while the remarkable session drummer Jim Keltner was recording (the man has credits for miles—John Lennon, Bob Dylan, you name it), Rufus piped up with an idea. Jon calmly stopped the session and invited Rufus for lunch. Rufus thought this was normal and happily accompanied his producer somewhere nice, where Jon proceeded to tell him that he was not to speak to the musicians and that, actually, if he wanted to talk to Jon in the future, he should go through his assistant, and maybe even his lawyer. Rufus was shocked and put off. Jon clearly was a bit of an asshole.

On the one hand, my brother was having the time of his life. On the other hand, I can't imagine it was much fun to be shunned by your producer, especially when you're only a kid doing his first album. It took two years, dozens of songs, and more than fifty reels of tape, but the two of them made something wonderful in the end. Rufus has always been protected in some strange, mystical way; a few times our aunt Anna has claimed he has a guardian angel. But he's also his own angel, strong-willed and super tough. He has had to be, maybe. I think he was likely more affected by our parents' divorce than I was, being a few years older than me, and he had to survive being put down for being gay, and had to fight for his career, working hard and succeeding at it, too, while still doing exactly what he wanted to do artistically and making the overtly uncommercial somehow commercial. While Kate was always in his corner when it came to most things, and especially his music, our dad didn't really get what Rufus was up to, and unfortunately didn't hide that from Rufus. Loudon was the one to pass along the demo that got Rufus signed, but my dad and Rufus have always been competitive, even though they aren't really in the same ring in the same fight. At least in Los

Angeles, Rufus had Lenny on his side. Whereas my father was incredibly hard on Rufus—too hard—Lenny loved him and showered him with praise.

Dan came with me on some of these trips; he knew LA well, having worked there for some years as a tennis instructor. Watching Rufus and Dan hang out was always a trip—two egomaniacs vying for attention. Their styles of music and way of making records couldn't have been more different, but they both wanted to rule the world. When they went at it, I was reminded how, in the company of men like this, women are oftentimes made to feel as if they don't exist. (Rufus used to make me feel like that a lot, but these days, it's the opposite: he makes me feel like doing more with my artistry. I appreciate him for that. He's even been quoted saying that I am one of the best living female singers. Maybe he's trying to make up for the past—he said one time that he'd never seen anyone who could be so beautiful and so ugly at the same time as me—but I also like to think he believes that I am one of the best.)

One night, outside the Akbar, a great little gay bar in Silverlake where we often hung out, Dan and I got into his car, Rufus got into his, and they drove into each other, the whole time laughing madly and maniacally. It was a ridiculous test of power and strength, like some drag race out of a James Dean movie where both boys are determined, even destined, to annihilate each other. Afterward, they waved goodbye and drove off in opposite directions.

Rufus may have just been starting out, but he had a major

leg up—a big record deal, a big producer, big ambition, and great songs. Dan, for his part, kept trying to catch a wave that always just eluded him, despite his talent and drive.

When Dan's tour came to an end, he moved into the Carlton Arms Hotel on East Twenty-Fifth Street in New York. At sixty bucks a night, and even lower weekly and monthly rates, it was home base for some junkies and old half-dying people, as well as wandering minstrels. Each room had been decorated by an okay-but-usually-not-great artist and most had shared bathrooms. Some rooms you could also rent by the hour, I eventually discovered.

After a time, it became clear Dan was losing interest in me. At one point, he urged me to go back to Montreal for a while. When I did, he stopped picking up my calls, until the one time he answered only to tell me to stay in Montreal. I took a bus to New York to try to change his mind but, instead, he introduced me to his girlfriend, an actor/dancer on Broadway— a chorus girl, essentially—who was older than me and way more together. When we met outside the Carlton Arms on a hot August afternoon, I found myself nervously climbing some scaffolding on the front of the building like a child in a schoolyard. Before me was a woman with an apartment, a job, confidence, and happiness. I wasn't going to win a contest against her. Dan had moved on. I needed to go cry, and the Carlton Arms let me rent a room for the afternoon in order to do it. (Thanks, guys.)

Heartbroken, I took the bus back to Montreal, where I funneled all my hurt and insecurity into songwriting and eating.

But a change was coming and someone else would soon step into my life to help me tremendously, a manager and producer named Nick Hill who had gotten his hands on *Ground Floor*, a ten-song cassette of my music that was floating around. Two of the songs, "Gone-to-Sea" and "Laurel & Hardy," some lyrics from the latter here, are about Rufus: *Three years before me you came out and cried / Boy, not a girl, where'd you get all that goddamn pride / You are so very thin and I've always wanted to fit into your pants.* One time, when Rufus and I were on the road in Japan, he told me that he made me, and that I would be nothing without him. Rufus was drunk. I was too, no doubt. I can see now why he believed that. But things would change. Also on that cassette was my mom's favorite song of mine, "Don't Forget," about the Montreal boyfriend I had left for Dan.

On the cover, there's a picture of me sitting on the stoop of my ground-floor apartment on Querbes. My mother was the one who had given me the money to put the songs down over a couple of days in Pierre Marchand's beautiful, woodsy, mountainside studio in Morin-Heights; Pierre had produced *Heartbeats Accelerating* and went on to wild success as Sarah McLachlan's cowriter and producer. Kate even registered the name Querbeservice to serve as the label (*Querbes* is pronounced "curb"). I can see her face now, beaming with pride at the thought of all of us being in the family business and running a type of folkie Brill Building where we would all write and sell our songs, press our own records, and achieve great success.

But the truth is that running a label is hard and neither Kate nor I had the business skills or the mindset to do it. Case in point, at the sessions, I remember feeling very lucky to be having so much fun while technically "working." It was my first time in a studio alone, with no mother or brother telling me what to do, and I was there with that on-again, off-again first boyfriend playing bass somewhat proficiently, and my cousin Lily and my friend Ariel on vocals. I played electric guitar, out of tune, and all I can say is thank heavens Tom Mennier was playing the right chords, one of the only real musicians involved. I still don't know if it is a great recording, but I think we somehow captured some magic in the mountains.

A few months later, what felt inevitable finally happened. I left my home on Querbes and moved full-time to New York to pursue music. I may still have been sad and insecure, but I was also hopeful—broken but running.

Five

I'VE ALWAYS LIKED THE WAY New York smells. Is it the hot wet pavement, the scent of desperation, or the smell of success that gets me?

I have met a few people who became wildly successful there, but mostly I know people who are just trying to survive in a place where that's difficult to do. In New York, life seems short, maybe because you can feel the velocity at which you're traveling. Of course, there are people who take calming walks in Central Park every day and go regularly to yoga classes or get their hair and nails done once a week, but I only know a few of those. Most of the people of my acquaintance carry around an instrument on their way to a gig or a camera on their way to a shoot or a last drink on their way to the next bar. These days I wake up earlier, but when I was young and in New York, I went to bed just before the sun rose—praying I'd fall asleep before the light caught me in whatever compromising position I might happen to be in—and woke up at noon.

When I got to New York, I started playing the guitar every day and just generally trying harder. Of course, it's a big town with a lot of people working to be seen and heard, and it was more difficult to stand out there than it had been in Montreal. But I began playing gigs regularly, carrying my guitar around with foolish pride, and taking one beating after another. I had crushes on everyone, but none of the men I liked seemed to like me back. And I continued to wrestle with real insecurity about my looks. I found it devastating that I was thought of as handsome, at best.

Lovesickness and jealousy had brought me to New York, but there was an actual person who lured me there, too—Nick Hill. Nick was, and still is, a serious musicophile, as well as a great friend and supporter of artists and musicians. I found my way to him through Penny Arcade, a New York performance artist I knew through my parents, who was the one who had given him my *Ground Floor* cassette. I remember first going to Penny's loft in Alphabet City when I was twelve or thirteen, with Rufus and my mom. It was in one of those prewar industrial New York buildings with no doorbell, occupied mostly by artists, some of them a little strung out, maybe. To get in, you had to yell up from the street and she'd throw down the key in a sock.

My mom was in heaven, and very proud to bring us there. I remember on that first visit, Penny served us some crappy spaghetti in tin bowls, which we ate on our laps. She also stared into my eyes and asked me lots of questions, including what kind of music I liked. I guess she was trying to figure out if I was worth the effort, and I must have passed the test because Penny was always very warm to me. The year I lived with him,

Dad took me to see Penny's show *Bitch! Dyke! Faghag! Whore!*
I loved it. There we were in some downtown theater space,
watching this cute, funny, brilliant, completely naked person
on a swing slinging one-liners into the audience and talking
about her first sexual experiences. To me, she represented an
ideal of edginess I could never attain—I'm more folksy. (But,
boy, did I try.) She was a big part of the LGBTQ community
in New York, and I know she also took Rufus under her wing
when he first started spending time there in the midnineties,
which really was a help to him given that our mother continued
to have some trouble totally accepting that part of him, much
as she tried.

Penny gave Nick my cassette, and after hearing it, he reached
out to me in Montreal. Nick had a number of things on the
go, including his own label, some "green" business initiative
that involved a small office in Manhattan, hosting a radio show
on WFMU, the seminal hipster radio station in the area, and
managing and working with the Dream Syndicate, Michael
Hurley, and Victoria Williams. Soon he took me on as well.

He and I had spoken on the phone a bunch of times, but the
first time I met him in person was after a showcase of young
female singers, called Nightingales, he had booked me on at
the Bottom Line in Greenwich Village. I knew the Bottom
Line well. In some senses, it was one of the places where I grew
up—a place of songwriters, young and old, some less known
and many famous. My parents had both played there, and so
had Suzzy and her sisters. I had sung on its stage as a kid, as
part of a Roches Christmas show when I was eight and also

with my parents. Nick soon got me my first residency, a weekly spot at a super-hip club also called Nightingales.

Nick wasn't at all what I expected. He is from Portland, Oregon, and he looked more like a lumberjack than a downtown New York music guy. He didn't wear black, he wore brown—a brown photographer's vest with a little foulard for a splash of color, Carhartt pants, and clogs. Right away I recognized a kindred spirit, and I gained a mentor, guide, and friend. Someone who could teach me not just about how to play music, but also how to feel about myself and how to act toward other people. Nick was, and still is, like another big brother to me, possibly a father figure, too. During those early years in the city, he took care of me without judgment.

The artists that he gravitated toward or those who gravitated toward him were, like me, a sometimes unhappy, emotional, and restless bunch. I remember a moving evening spent with Vic Chestnutt at Bob Mould's loft, and nights at Mary Margaret O'Hara's dark mansion in Toronto. We went to see Victoria Williams out in Pioneertown, a surreal desert outpost near Joshua Tree in California, and visited with Garth Hudson and his wife, Maud, in Woodstock. They were real night owls and only rose at four in the afternoon to play polka on an accordion and create poetry soundscapes on the computer. These were the elders of the movement and the outsiders of their musical generation. They were revered, especially by younger artists.

Nick brought me to play on the West Coast, too, and we stayed with strung-out hipsters in Portland, sleeping on the floors of houses with busted-out windows. I met so many bands and musicians, I can't remember their names, all of whom were surviving on the margins of the fucking shitty music business. Diehards, dedicated and foolish artists, dreamers.

I stayed, on and off, with Nick and his wife, Alex, and their toddler, Isaac, in their house on Eighth Street at Havemeyer. Their home became my home, and the way they lived and treated each other had a big influence on me. Alex had once been a ballet dancer and a painter, but now was a full-time homemaker. The two of them are much calmer and more easygoing than I am, and I really appreciated the world they created. They also demonstrated to me that marriage could work. They were (and still are) a united front. They are also really granola, and I say that lovingly.

Their place overflowed with plants for making herbal tinctures, and fancy creams from the health-food store, and veggies from the big roof garden that Alex tended. There was always a pot of quinoa going or burdock root braising on the stove, and active cultures coming to life on top of the fridge. All their kids (they would have three) were born at home, wore cloth diapers, were homeschooled, and had long hair and sprouts coming out their ears.

In contrast to the frantic energy of New York, their home had a slower, softer pace. I may be glorifying Nick and Alex's marriage, but whatever problems they had, they kept them from me. I did notice that they weren't terribly physical toward each other in front of people. They weren't cold, but they weren't touchy-feely either. One day, after

Alex heard the news that one of her grandparents had died, she leapt into Nick's arms, bawling like a little girl, and I remember burly, barrel-chested Nick holding her very closely and lovingly. It was a window into their private tenderness that I found very moving. I felt like I was now part of a family with two loving parents.

Not that I'd actually trade the parents I had. Once, in the summer just after I'd moved to New York, Kate decided to cycle all the way from Montreal to see me. On a hot day, she got aboard her ten-speed and pushed off. She didn't tell anyone or make any plans or preparations, and she didn't bring anything with her, aside from an old army-surplus backpack with metal clips that dug into her shoulders. She wore clogs and cut-off jeans. No phone.

Jack Kerouac was one of her heroes, and she'd always yearned for the road and potentially dangerous adventure. (She was very interested in Kerouac's Quebec roots and the relationship he had with his French Canadian mother. At forty-seven, the age at which Kerouac had died, she embraced his spirit and wrote a musical based on his life.) My mother, in midlife, free of her children and the demands of domesticity, blossomed even more as an artist and individual. I was always impressed by that, although at the time I admit I found it annoying, too. Stunts like these? My mother's need for attention always got in the way of my own need for attention. Even in her late forties and fifties, when she walked into a room, she outshone me and everyone there.

After about a hundred miles on her bike, Kate knew she wasn't going to be able to pedal all the way to Nick Hill's door, which is where I was living at the time. So she checked into a B and B for a night's sleep and the next day managed to make it to Ticonderoga, New York, where she and her bike caught a train to Penn Station. When I picked her up, I could have killed her, and might have if she weren't so exhausted, the backs of her legs sunburned and her hands covered with blisters. (It turns out those silly bike gloves exist for a reason.) I remember her pedaling down the sidewalk toward me as I waited at the wheel of Nick's car on Eighth Avenue. As she got close, she flung one leg over to meet the other and coasted, looking as proud and rebellious as a teenager. We couldn't fit the bike in Nick's little car, so she drove the car back to Brooklyn while I followed behind her on the bike. It was a hot summer night. When we got home, Nick poured her a whiskey and even let her smoke in the house, something he never allowed with anybody else.

Every time Kate came to New York in those early days, she would really go for it. She couldn't resist the excitement of the city. We'd stay out late, going to shows, getting into trouble. I saw firsthand some of her wild spirit. One hot September night after watching the San Gennaro festival on Havemeyer Street, we went around to a few bars on Nick's old Dutch carrier bike, which had a big cart in the front for kids or wood or whatever, careening through the empty streets, laughing. She ended up falling into a pile of smelly trash. She pulled her soiled dress off over her head and walked home to Nick's without it. It was a glimpse of what she had been like as a young woman.

Nights like those with my mom, and all the love and care I witnessed in Nick and Alex's home, did not save me from myself. My time as a young musician in New York was tormented, confusing, mistake-riddled, and incredibly fun. I would shoot myself in the foot and while trying to bandage it up, shoot myself in the other one. I stumbled over people and threw myself at others who pushed me away. I started drinking heavily and doing a lot of hard drugs. I put on fifteen pounds. I placed myself in risky situations—ones in which I could have lost my life—and somehow managed to extricate myself from them. It's all a bit of blur, looking back.

When I hung out with Nick, the focus was on music and making connections and friends. Nick had been a cab driver in New York, and the two of us would drive everywhere in his old car, and really fast, too. Nick was completely unintimidated by parking in Manhattan and could find a spot anywhere. Sometimes he would force his car into an empty space by pushing against the cars parked in front of and behind us, literally shifting them to accommodate his little Honda. He always knew what was going on, and where. Sometimes we would go to see three or four shows a night.

Nick had a great way of walking into a bar. He would bypass the bouncer or the person collecting money, claiming he was with the band or that he was needed backstage. The best part about this strategy was that we were able to catch a small part of someone's gig, but not the whole thing. I didn't want to sit through an hour of some songwriter in a small club somewhere. I wanted to hear what other people were doing, but really mostly so I could compare it to my own.

Many years later, Nick reminded me of how reluctant and ambivalent I was about making music that would appeal to more people. I know I had no interest in pleasing the record labels or giving them something they wanted—to the point that I sabotaged every potential record deal. On nights when people "of consequence" were in the audience, I would get fatally fucked up. It would take me a long time to turn this tendency around.

Today, being on the periphery of what can sell is something that people accept and even like about me, but back then it was awful. The music industry was collapsing, and I was all over the place myself, stylistically and emotionally. Even when I was sort of pleased that a label showed interest in me—Rough Trade, Warners, Columbia, or whatever—I could never deliver a sure thing. But I was well aware that my parents had both been on major labels, and Rufus was now on DreamWorks, so the idea of my music being released courtesy of Catbutt Records (my ex-husband's nickname for little labels) was mortifying. I created an impossible situation for myself. I was afraid to fail but I kept setting myself up to fail.

Then there was the other area of my life where I also set myself up to fail. A couple of weeks after I met Nick, he introduced me to a guy named Phil, and I immediately fell in love with him. Everyone else also lost it for Phil, so I had lots of company. He has the honor of being the first of a few men I loved who didn't love me back (at least for a little while). It was my blue period. After being crushed by Dan Bern, I was damaged, but also loud, able to get up and sing anywhere, not in a girlish, demure manner, but more brazenly. This probably turned some men off as much as it may have intrigued others.

Phil was from Dublin, a slightly guilty Protestant from the upper-middle classes who had come to America in the early nineties in hopes of making it as a musician. His band, Those Bleeding Tulips, had had some success back home and he wanted to be a rock star, but he was working in construction and carpentry to pay the bills. He had such a heavy Irish accent, I could barely make out what he was saying at first, but that might also have had something to do with the way Phil spoke, in wild bursts of ideas, or how many pints he'd had. Phil was also well read, and I didn't always understand his literary references, though who knows, he could have just been making them up.

Phil introduced me to music I'd never listened to before, darker and heavier stuff—Television, Joy Division, the Ramones, Nick Cave and the Bad Seeds, the Melvins. I traipsed after him through the streets of the East Village and Williamsburg, drinking during the day and doing hard drugs and pills at night. Phil's dream was to be an Irish poet in the streets of New York, a new, edgier, good-looking Shane MacGowan. Seemed impossible to pull off. The first night we met set the pattern: I followed Phil from bar to bar, one Irish haunt after another. They all melded into each other, there were so many—Scratcher, Mona's, 2A, Manitoba's, Arlene's Grocery, GPT, the Levee—a blur of bartenders and free drinks, with the action revolving around what was playing on the jukebox.

Phil loved to perform, but the few times I saw him play, he fumbled onstage, having drunk too much before going on. He was a bunch of years older than me, and by the time I met him he seemed done with his own music on some level. But he was a big supporter of mine and looked to me to keep trying. I felt I wanted to make it, for me and for him.

After a few months of me chasing after him, Phil told me he had a spare room in his apartment on Metropolitan Avenue in Williamsburg, and that I was welcome to move in if I wanted. I made it my new life's mission.

Two or three days after I got there, a girl with clothespins in her hair began showing up outside the building. Phil's apartment was illegal (he pulled the electricity and utilities from the neighbors) and didn't have a doorbell, so she would simply yell for him from the sidewalk. *Who is this strange woman, moving in on my dream life with this big drunk Irish musician/carpenter?*

She turned out to be Mercedes Grower from London, a complete one of a kind. A traveler, ex-addict, troublemaker, dancer, and comedienne, she would become a good friend forever. It seems that during some previous drunken evening, Phil had promised Mercedes the room, too, and now she had nowhere to go. From that point on, we split the rent three ways. Mercedes got the tiny room with the door. I took the living room, and Phil literally contorted his six-foot-four frame in order to sleep inside a closet. It was a young people's apartment without the IKEA. The walls were painted with murals, and everything was flea market, handmade, or from the trash, with foreign money in the catch-all bowls, multiple electric and acoustic guitars, kimonos and scarves, rose-tinted glasses, overflowing ashtrays, and plenty of drugs. We sweltered in the summer and froze in the winter. The good news is that there weren't any cockroaches. That was more of a Manhattan problem. We had mice instead.

At the time, Mercedes was going through a terrible breakup. She spent almost every day on the phone with friends, pacing between her bed and the tiny kitchen, through my room (the living room). She would also regularly call her mother or sister back home in London, conversations that would almost always devolve into screaming matches surprisingly quickly, with Mercedes stomping around like a madwoman, in her underpants or without. In fact, Mercedes was naked a lot of the time, and so was Phil. I was always waking up or coming home to someone's bare bum or schlong hanging out. When Mercedes wasn't walking around naked, chain-smoking, she would take baths. Emerging from the water, she would wrap only her hair in a towel.

Looking back, I guess she just wanted people to know she was there. And, oh, did I ever know it. Despite being a small woman, her personality was big and her heart was warm. The two of us were a funny pair. More striking than pretty, with long black hair and dark eyes, a strong nose, and slightly crooked teeth, Mercedes was musky and sensuous. What was I? Right, I was big and handsome.

Whenever Phil stayed out all night, or sometimes all week on a bender, Mercedes and I would hole up in the apartment, licking our wounds like a pair of sad females waiting for the returning soldier, brother, lover. After a while, we forgot men altogether and had ourselves a grand old time.

If Phil was around, I would pass the day by playing the guitar, and then he and I would meet up somewhere at cocktail hour to go see a show or two or three. We'd hang backstage, barhop around the East Village until 4 a.m. when management kicked us out, and then go home for food and a few more cigs and a joint, at which point we'd try to shut our eyes to the sun beginning to show its beautiful sci-fi light through the window, the scary giant trucks on Metropolitan Avenue already screaming by.

I thought I wanted his love, but what Phil gave me was much more valuable. He gave me friendship. He believed in my music. He gave me something to write about, and to pine for.

He and Nick were the two main men in my life. I would say that Nick probably saved me. I went through a period when I was sniffing and smoking heroin. Of course, Nick noticed and pulled me aside one night at Max Fish, on Ludlow Street, for a little talk. He could see that my eyes were pinned and I was antsy. He told me that if I kept on doing heroin, he was going to tell Rufus and Kate. It worked. I wasn't a teenager. I wasn't afraid that my mom would come get me and take me home.

I was more embarrassed and afraid of disappointing them. Afraid of them finding out how much time I was wasting.

In my experience, some drugs can be mind-expanding and fun, but heroin just turns you off. A light goes out, and you don't care anymore. I certainly never wrote any songs on heroin. I just watched TV or hung out, if you can call it that, on a couch, either with friends or complete strangers. My natural state is to care too much. I'm the opposite of blasé, and I'm generally a fan of frantic energy. Of course, being that way, I totally get the allure of heroin. All your worries melt away and nothing matters, which eventually becomes a problem, too. Though people around me shot up heroin, I never did. I found it too scary. Maybe that's why I was able to walk away from it so easily. I was wild but also sensible—or maybe I just didn't want to spend half my life asleep. Anyway, when I wasn't totally wasting my time in a gutter somewhere, I would often head over to Nick's, my safe hippie haven, and he and I would listen to music all night. The quinoa called, thank god.

Around that same time, Nick was compiling an album of songs that Jeff Buckley had performed on Nick's WFMU radio show. The two of them were close and Nick was very involved in his career. Jeff had drowned just a year before I'd arrived in New York. People revered him and were deeply affected by his death. Jeff's music hadn't been on my radar, but if I had met him, I'm sure I would have fallen in love with him like everyone else did.

After he died, there was a void in the East Village that a

lot of other musicians tried to fill. Myself included. But the world wasn't ready (maybe still isn't) to bow down to a girl. Even Rufus had trouble getting a gig at Sin-é, where Jeff had reigned. I know Rufus was keenly aware of the power Jeff had over people. Rufus had lived in Queens briefly in the mid-nineties and had spent time in the East Village with Jeff.

Even though Jeff was gone, there were still plenty of charismatic young men to fall in love with. I stumbled through those streets, forlorn and lovesick a lot of the time. My heart rose up out of me with such power for beautiful men in darkened doorways, sharing a cigarette, or on an old couch in the corner of a smoky room. On the edges of the rooftops of strangers' buildings. In the back seats of cars, and at sunrise on the banks of the East River, where a diner is the only place to go because it's too late to go to bed.

Some of my crushes were stronger than others. I had a couple of relationships, but I didn't seem to be what men wanted. They seemed to be looking for someone more waifish and ethereal. Someone quieter, less disturbing. Someone more beautiful, stylish, more controlled, more organized. Less drink-y, less needy. Someone who kissed less hard. I'm still not that person.

Six

It's hard for me to write about my music, but I'm going to try. I have trouble watching or even listening to myself. I can listen to my tracks in the studio, of course, and I write songs for hours on end and have to listen back to the recordings I make as I go, but I don't always like what I hear or see. Actually, I don't think that's the point of music. I think it's a ride with twists and turns, ups and downs, and everything in between. Music is what you make as well as the thing that brings you to it and where it takes you. A place, a feeling, an experience, a country, a world.

Journalists often ask if music is something I was "made" to do—a warm-up question they use to break the ice and get me to talk about my family right away. The answer is yes, I *was* made to do it by my parents, but I liked it and I wanted the attention and the fun of performing. I was a misfit, and often unhappy, but singing and playing made me feel good. It was a big gamble to commit to it, though, because I wasn't naturally gifted. I don't hear music in my head, and I don't go around jotting down bits of lyrics on scraps of paper. I don't regularly practice, on my own or with other musicians. I don't play more than one instrument, even though I have sat at a piano a thousand times and tried to learn how to play. The same with drums and bass. I get intimidated.

Some singers can go into a studio and get it right, first time every time. Others need to toil at it. Some of the greatest singers are hardly singers at all—their pitch or rhythm is a little funny—but they get the song across perfectly. In my early years, I could hit the nail on the head sometimes and other times I had to wrestle with the notes. Either my voice was as clear as a bell or it was shredded from smoking and overuse. Once in a while, no sound came out at all, which was frightening. But after a good few years of touring and a couple of records, my voice grew more honed and I learned to take better care of it. There was no doubt a psychological aspect to the raggedness, too. When I was afraid or sad or intimidated, my voice could fail me. Other times, it saved me.

One person's voice is handed to them like a gift. Another person has to create a voice, literally, in her gut, her heart, her throat. Some people seem to channel someone else's voice, taking it on and welcoming it. Your body is your own but sometimes it's also a tool for someone else to come through. Sometimes singing feels like a skill and sometimes it feels like an art. Singing has saved my life. Sometimes I feel that if it weren't for being able to sing, I would not be here. I would have died by misadventure or taken my own life. But that might be a load of cow shit. I can really sit in sadness, as you might have guessed, but I can get out of it pretty easily, too, often by singing.

When it comes to my songwriting, I can't help but compare it to my parents'. I feel that Kate's music has a lyrical subtlety that mine lacks. She was way better at referencing history and philosophy in her lyrics. She could also play her instruments better than I play the guitar, and she's written more iconic songs that other artists have covered. My father is perhaps the most underrated songwriter of his generation (that's what my mom would say, when she was feeling generous). Once when I was a kid, my mom took me to see a huge Led Zeppelin show at Montreal's Forum, and I remember Robert Plant talking to me afterward about how great my dad was, saying, "Your dad's a fucking genius," his British accent and his stunning look making him very convincing. I was only ten at the time, and my response was "I know." Loudon's voice and words should put him somewhere in the pantheon of male self-obsessed, overly sexed, witty, and whiny songwriters, but they often go unappreciated. He can distill complicated emotions beautifully into a three-minute song. (Some songs are better than others, of course; when you are as prolific as my dad is, not everything can be magic.)

The truth is, for the last twenty-five years I've made and played music and gotten good at it. The overall goal, I guess, is to enjoy playing but also to get to do it in front of millions of people. Most musicians want this, but the reality is more difficult and complicated. Recognition is essential for the ego, but you don't need recognition to play music. After all, it's a natural expression that has been commodified to produce a financial benefit. Some of the time, anyway.

Making money as an artist is an art in itself. One that has mostly eluded me. Maybe all careers are like this, but it seems to me that a lot of people in music either give up at some point, or else they find a way to make a living doing it. Did most of them start out wanting to be famous? Most likely. But not everyone can get there, since that would defeat the purpose of fame. I'm always surprised people come to my shows. I'm grateful and happy, and then I'm mad that more people didn't buy tickets or that the hall wasn't bigger. And then I get over it.

In 1999, Nick introduced me to most of the musicians who would become my musical brothers for the next few years. We played gigs and made a couple of EPs of the songs I wrote by myself in my room on the guitar. This way of writing and making music defined me as an artist—a solo act, but one who also plays and shares a musical language with many musicians.

One of them was George Javori, the drummer who played on my first EP, *6 Songs*. He was a half-gypsy, half-Hungarian Jew, born in 1972, who had fled his homeland with his mother when he was a child. I say "was" because George is one of the only people I've known well who killed himself. He and his mother arrived in New York with only a few dollars to their name. George was proud of her, and of everything they had been through together in order to survive, but it clearly weighed on him, too.

He was small and boyish, with soft dark skin, and he wore a Star of David around his neck and a hoop earring in one ear. When he played, he sometimes took off his shirt, and the way he glistened behind the drums like some sort of skin-slick angel was something to see. I slept with him once, but mostly we liked to make out. I can remember how his hot mouth tasted and how his tongue moved in mine. We took long walks in Brooklyn and listened to the radio in his car. Some nights he insisted on playing Captain Beefheart endlessly, trying my patience so much I would roll over in his bed and go to sleep. I loved him, but I didn't realize he was suicidal, which makes me feel like a bad friend. After attempting to kill himself a few times in different ways (secrets he kept from everyone), he succeeded in 2005.

My piano-playing friend from Montreal, Tom Mennier, wild and kooky and talented, came down to New York to play with us. We had Andrew Hall on bass, Jimi Zhivago on guitar, and Doug Wieselman sitting in occasionally on clarinet and sax. Jimi and Doug were already New York music-scene legends. I forged an important musical relationship with Doug in particular, who would go on to play on all my records. David Mansfield, a top-notch session musician I'd known since I was a little kid because he had played with my dad, also contributed on a couple of songs, along with Duke McVinnie, another great talent. I felt extremely lucky that they all seemed to like my songs and were respectful of me and my ideas.

We got good results, too—a little live-sounding, but that was the spirit we were after, or at least the one we created. These musicians weren't a band in the strictest definition of the word, though, because I would play with anyone, anytime, if they wanted to play with me and they seemed interesting. Maybe it was my replacement for not having an actual relationship—I had as many musical partners as possible! No loyalty to a single bass player or drummer, just trying everyone out. Which is what people really hear on my records, for better or for worse.

Along with the regular players on these early projects, various people would drop in: John Schumann, an old friend who made his own pedals and had crazy sounds; the amazing underground rock cellist Jane Scarpantoni; Teddy Thompson on vocals, along with Kate and Anna and Lily; and sometimes friends who were amateur musicians, so why not see what they could do? Looking back, maybe I *did* take it too far with the amateurs. If you listen to a song like "Jimi," it sounds like everyone is just trying to keep up with one another.

I also liked to change up the tunings. Unlike the open tuning used by many artists (Joni Mitchell, Keith Richards, and countless blues and jazz musicians), I made mine up almost arbitrarily. I'd always felt limited by my guitar playing, so I would tune the strings up or down, just to hear what might happen. This added to the quirkiness of the music and made it all the more difficult to put a finger on what exactly my style was. I was trying to hit a moving target, or maybe be a moving target. Rather than homing in and crafting a sound by removing things or making clear musical choices, I kept experimenting.

A few years ago, I listened to my first EP again, and the difference in the feel of each song is staggering. I remember I even rerecorded some of them a couple of times, ending up with different versions floating around, which Nick and I would just release, because…why not?

It probably wasn't the best strategy for success, but I certainly enjoyed trying out different ways of recording and making music. I still didn't know what kind of performer I wanted to be, other than more edgy than my folk-musician parents. I wish I could have been more avant-garde or even just "of the moment," but my songwriting was particular, personal, and steeped in the past.

After Rufus's debut was finally released, he received a lot of critical acclaim. Thank god for that, really, because around this time I was able to live off the cash I made selling my EPs when I was the opening act at Rufus's shows. Once Rufus was playing big venues, I could make six or seven hundred dollars a night this way; after all, no one could find my music in stores. I had the CDs pressed by a guy in Harlem who worked out of his apartment. I'd order a few hundred at a time and drive uptown every couple of weeks to pick them up in his parking lot. I created the artwork and stuffed the CDs by myself or with friends.

Rufus and I fought a lot, as we always tended to do back then, but we also had a good time. There is a photograph that someone took of the two of us asleep in a tiny hotel room. The sun is coming up, and each of us is sprawled out on a twin bed, shirtless, on our stomach, like two children. Our hair is the same length, and it falls over our shoulders. You can hardly tell which one is me and which is Rufus, or who's the boy and who's the girl. Rufus and I don't look that much alike, but sometimes we feel like the same person. Even though our lives and characters are so different, even though we fought a lot as small children before becoming closer as teenagers, then losing touch a bit in our twenties but coming together again since our mom died and needing each other more, there is something that makes us the same. Maybe a lot of siblings feel this. Connected forever.

I don't know if you're wondering where my dad was during those New York years, but at the time I was wondering, too. I saw him every now and then for dinner, and once he gave me maybe two hundred bucks (he was usually a little tight with money, maybe trying to teach me a lesson). When I was late with the rent one time, I got a loan from one of his generous friends, not from him, and paid it back right away.

I asked Loudon recently about that time (after many years of discontent, things have gotten better between us). He told me he'd been jealous of Nick Hill, because Nick had taken me under his wing when my dad simply couldn't. Loudon said he thought I'd chosen well in Nick, that Nick was more open to who I was, whereas Loudon would have wanted to push me to do things his way. Boiling it down, he was basically telling me that he stayed away from me in my early twenties because he felt he couldn't influence me, and that he was sad about that. I've noticed that Loudon often retreats when he's most needed. Still, he made it sound as though he recognized that I was good—or *could* be good—at music. He didn't come right out and say it, but I think that's what he meant. If only I had known at the time.

Between 1999 and 2002, along with opening or singing backup for Rufus, I would sometimes open for my dad. The times I remember best are when the two of us went on short tours, once in the States and another for two weeks in the UK. We would be strained and uncomfortable at the beginning of each tour, like two people who didn't know each other. But by the end, I was always sad to go home. I loved my mother, and I feel really lucky to be her daughter, but in truth, I feel a little bit robbed of the relationship I could have had with my dad. Of course, it wasn't all Kate's fault. Loudon could have come to visit us in Canada or insisted we come see him more wherever he was living. I didn't really grow up around him, so only a part of me saw him as a father. The other part saw him as another man to disappoint. To be rejected by.

On the road with him, I was impressed but also unimpressed. He lived the life of the traveling solo musician, which was already my reality but also offered a preview of my future. I spent a lot of my time waiting backstage to come on, waiting for his set to be done, waiting for a lift back to the hotel. Watching my dad but mostly watching myself, in the wings of those old music halls in England. Smoking, drinking, looking at myself in the mirror in those shabby, gawdy, tiny backstages where you're surrounded by the ghosts of countless singers, actors, and dancers who had waited there for their moment, too. I felt a part of a long line of people of the stage... and it wasn't a bad feeling, just a little tiring. Sometimes I felt like I had been a working musician forever, though I was only twenty-four.

One night in one of those old music halls, I decided to watch my dad's show rather than stare at myself in the mirror until my cue. I went up the stairs past the first balcony and found a little empty loge, high up in the corner of the theater. Loudon was having a good show, as usual, in front of a captivated and loving audience.

Then he got to a song I knew—well, I knew all of them. Maybe I should say he got to a song I didn't like. I'd always thought it was a bit stupid and mean-spirited, but more than that, I felt bad for its subject. It's called "I'd Rather Be Lonely" and he sings it to a woman—a girlfriend, I had always assumed. In the introduction that night, though, he was cracking jokes, all jolly, and announced to the audience that the song was about me—his daughter—and the year we had lived together. I was shocked and totally offended and embarrassed. Did he mean it? Could it be true? Did he realize I was listening?

Every night I get the blues
Greens and yellows and chartreuses
You're still living here with me, I'd rather be lonely
All the time I look around
For excuses to leave town
Everybody wants somebody, but I'd rather be lonely
Loneliness is happiness, it takes less than two
I confess that I digress from it when I'm with you
Let's us make a brand-new start

Separate and stay apart
I've had enough having and holding
I'd rather be lonely
I think that I need some space
Every day you're in my face
How can I get rid of you, I'd rather be lonely

Up there in my loge, I began to cry, and as I did, I thought of another of his lyrics that had always hurt me: *When you cry, you're just a clone of every woman I have ever known.* A part of me wanted to jump to my death from my tiny seat or, better yet, take off into the night, leaving him standing there waiting for me. But the show must go on, so I dried my tears and went down the stairs and on to the stage and sang "Dead Skunk" with him, looking to stress any discordant harmony that could possibly make the song more interesting.

But really, such a reaction was a culmination of years of sadness about him and my mom splitting up, as well as my own feelings about myself. I know that my dad wanted the best for me, and that he liked my songs well enough, and that he was proud of me in a way, given that I was hard to be proud of because I was prone to failures and missteps and self-sabotage.

I think, at times, I shocked and surprised him in my own right. Often, I was very exposed and vulnerable onstage and yet also crass and loud. My music was different, my voice was wild, and my appearance was out of control. I made him feel worried and uncomfortable, which was not hard to do given that he is a conservative man in many ways, reticent in the face of other people's pain and suffering. Considering all that he's done, he's gotten through life relatively unscathed, a testament to putting yourself first. Though he would soon learn what it's like to be on the other side of a mean song.

I guess I've learned a lot from my dad.

Seven

I'VE NEVER HAD A REAL JOB, except working at a coffee shop the summer I was fifteen and tending bar briefly at the Sarajevo. Music has always been the way I supported myself, except for a stretch of time when I was seventeen and Kate handed over to me the monthly child support check she received from my father, in hopes that I'd learn how to spend and save money. By the time I was twenty-five in New York, I was playing three or four nights a week in different small venues in the city, as well as going out to the West Coast from time to time to perform at places like the Silverlake Lounge, Largo, the Knitting Factory, Berbati's Pan in Portland, Oregon, and the Crocodile and the Tractor Tavern in Seattle. Coffeehouses and clubs. It was all fairly low-rent—I was still staying on people's couches—but it was fun, too. Rufus was touring his second record, *Poses*, extensively, so I also sang backup and often did the opening slot, selling my EPs from the merch table.

My brother, who had always liked to party, was partying even harder, and I was right there alongside him. But I was becoming restless to do my own thing. I felt like I was running from a shadow, if that means anything. The shadow of my family, and the darkness of my own self-destructive behavior. I had that chip on my shoulder that my mother hated, and I didn't want it anymore. So many people believed in me, and it was time to start believing in myself.

When does someone's music career really begin? When you stand in front of an auditorium full of parents and classmates at the talent show as a kid? When you sing along with your mother? Is it about getting noticed or is it about making money? Well, for me at least, my career only really began after I made my third EP, the one with the song "Bloody Mother Fucking Asshole" on it. I guess, in many ways, though I tried to learn from his discipline, that's how my father helped my career.

I was angry at him in a number of the classic ways a daughter in her twenties can be angry at a dad who wasn't really there for her growing up, and also because of the way he questioned my legitimacy as a singer-songwriter—I feared he might be right. When I saw him for our rare dinners, he would ask me what I was doing with my time, and I would attempt to justify my existence, not a pleasant experience. But he also challenged me as a songwriter because he himself is so frank in his own songs. I was mad at him, sure, but I was also just mad. Mad at men. Mad at myself.

Once, I stupidly told a journalist that Loudon inspired "BMFA," and it's been really hard to correct the narrative. (I've been way too open with journalists at times, and I've gotten bitten in the ass as a result.) But I'll say it here: the song is not "about" my dad. He was just the springboard, though he also became one of the targets. Though I was a "daughter of" twice over, doors seemed closed to me, in stark contrast to the attention paid to the "sons of" musical stars. I knew and hung out with all those boys, in New York and LA: Teddy Thompson, Sean Lennon, Chris Stills, Harper Simon, and the list goes on and on. I liked them—these were my friends—but they were all getting signed and written about and had publicists and photo shoots and beautiful girlfriends. Were their songs better than mine? Were their songs more genuine? I think "Bloody Mother Fucking Asshole" is really about getting the short end of the stick.

I wrote the music quickly and was practically finished with it when the lyrics at the end came out of my mouth. It's an earnest song, and as strident as it is vulnerable, and the coda really packs a punch. All those bloody mother fucking assholes. I wrote it out of misery, but it was also fun to sing. And very quickly after I started to perform it, it became an anthem for people who were mad at, or hurt by, someone. I know it sounds cheesy, but in some ways that's what separates "BMFA" from my other songs. Despite what people assume, it's not overly personal or particular to me.

I don't sing it much anymore unless there's a good reason to. These reasons may include "I want to dedicate this next song to the guy talking in the back" or, for a good long while, "This song is for Trump." That kind of thing. Audiences request it sometimes, but I'll only do it if it feels right. I never do it if my dad is in the audience, and I won't do it in front of a more conservative crowd, unless I'm a little pissed at them. (I'm grateful that so far my kids haven't started singing it, but I'm sure they will at some point.)

Around the time I wrote that song, Nick Hill needed to move on from managing me. His kids were getting older, and he had to find better-paying clients. When things started to fall apart between us, Nick asked that we sign a very basic agreement that if I released or otherwise made money from any of the recordings he and I had done together, he would receive some small compensation. I wish it was different—I'd always wanted to make him proud—but unfortunately Nick never made a cent on the music we created together.

Despite the sentiments I expressed in "BMFA," it's not that there was *no* interest in my music from connected people who could help me. I met with producers, labels, and other managers. Rick Chertoff (Cyndi Lauper, Joan Osborne) wanted me to rewrite all the songs with him, and I didn't want to do that. Joe Boyd (the McGarrigles, Nick Drake, Fairport Convention) saw me as a pure folk singer, and I didn't see myself that way. I walked away from all such opportunities because I was hardheaded and wanted my own story.

Eventually I saved up enough money to record my third EP, booking a few days in the Globe Studios on Thirteenth Street. I was without Nick, without any producer—just an engineer and a bunch of great musicians—and so I invited interested people to come in to give me advice. During one of the sessions, Donald Fagen of Steely Dan (always a champion of mine, along with his wife, Libby Titus) dropped in to hear how things were progressing. His visit coincided with the arrival of Brad Albetta, a bass player I had never worked with, who was going to play on the song "This Life" because the person I'd booked had had to leave for LA to play with Aimee Mann, his main gig. Brad, an incredibly gifted and natural musician, outdid himself that day, wanting to impress me—which he did—but I think also wanting to impress Donald.

I had met Brad a few weeks earlier, in the kitchen of a mutual musician friend, Cameron Greider. At some point, Brad walked in with his bass on his back, looking like a beautiful, lost, caged animal. He was also in need of immediate assistance. A singer he had been recording in his studio earlier that day had given him some OxyContin, which he had stupidly taken, not realizing what it was. His pale blue eyes were pinned, and though he was smiling, he looked a little afraid—he was late for a gig in the Village, and he didn't know how he was going to get there. That's when I came to the rescue. I had a friend's old blue van parked outside on the street, a formidable wreck of a vehicle with one hundred fifty thousand miles on it that we used mostly for carting around instruments and gear. I offered to drive him.

We raced across town, taking Houston, with me swerving through traffic with ease and aplomb, hoping to impress him. About four minutes later, I dropped him off right in front of the club. Since he still looked stunned and was also having trouble walking, I got out and helped him with his amp. I had fallen in love with the guy at first sight.

When I hired Brad for the session, I had no idea he was

a gifted bass player; I just wanted an excuse to see him again. Then he came in with his yellow short-scale bass and his yellow hair and he did something amazing.

So began my shameless pursuit, and why not: I was lonely and more than free. Dan was long gone, Phil wasn't able to love me back (given that he was an alcoholic who couldn't be with anyone at that point, especially not someone who drank; he had left town and was getting sober, thank goodness), and my old boyfriend was gone for good. Brad liked me well enough, but he also liked my music and saw an opportunity to work on a good project. When I ran out of money to pay for Globe Studios, Brad offered his own place, saying we could work on the record together in his spare time and that he wouldn't charge me a cent until we had licensed the record to a label.

Brad called his studio Monkey Boy, after an alter ego of his (he made a record of his own sad and angry music under that name). It was in a classic old factory building on Murray Street, practically a New York landmark, which dated back to the late 1800s. It was so close to the Twin Towers that after 9/11, Brad got some money for repairs from the relief fund. Out the giant windows in the control room you could see into people's apartments in the building across the street, once the city's main postal sorting office. Sonic Youth had their studio upstairs, and the rest of the building was rented to New York City Jam, a slightly cringey concept—for a small fee, business executives who played instruments could live their dreams, jamming after work. It made for a lot of blues licks wafting through the halls. A couple of doors down was the strip club New York Dolls, and though I knew girls who worked there, I never ventured inside.

At the time, Brad sometimes made me feel as though he was doing me a favor, but I was under his spell. Thirty-seven to my twenty-six, he was charming and strange, kind of a "tough" guy. Like me, he had been earning a living in music since the age of eighteen, first playing weddings and bar mitzvahs with his father's big band and then with New York City Swing, a pretty big outfit that toured all around the tristate area. Also like me, he was steeped in music from another era. On top of that, his parents were also divorced. His dad left when he was five, and would visit on weekends and in the summer, but his mom, Marion, was the one who raised him, working hard to bring up Brad, his twin brother, and his sister.

Yet in terms of family background, we were from separate planets. Brad was born in Flatbush to Italian American parents and grew up in Canarsie. When I met him, he was desperately trying to extricate himself from these roots. He told me that he'd always felt like an outsider in his deeply Italian American family. He had always been drawn to Manhattan, and to WASPy women. In me, I think he saw a sort of escape. He liked my mother and her music, and my brother's music, too, and he also liked the fact that I knew a lot of famous and talented musicians and artists. At first, and for a good while, my mother liked him back—Brad was very attractive and oddly charming, and his musical talent was undeniable. We were both titillated by his tales of being related to men in the mob, about his uncle "Nicky the Snake" and his other uncle, the crooked cop nicknamed "Blue-eyed Louie," and about the Lufthansa heist in *Goodfellas* being based on a family story. It seemed so clichéd, and yet at first I romanticized it. Later, it became less romantic, even depressing and a little scary.

While we were working on the songs that eventually became part of my self-titled debut album, I lived in the BedStuy neighborhood of Brooklyn and later in Williamsburg and would walk over the Brooklyn or Williamsburg Bridge to go to the studio, feeling lucky and happy. With the help of our friend Cameron, who played guitar, as well as Brian Fulk, the engineer, we wrestled the record into some sort of shape— which took two years because we could only work when Brad and the studio were available.

Recording wasn't always easy. Brad was tough on me when he thought I could do better; also, our musical tastes were different, which led to us toiling over every note. Sometimes Sonic Youth was a little loud and we had to withstand hour upon hour of feedback and monotonous bass notes from above. But that was forgivable, as Brad pointed out, because the band needed to play for a long while before the magic happened. No matter how tense our sessions sometimes were, I loved being at the studio, which was sprawling and messy and filled with dusty tchotchkes and cables and lots of broken gear. The elevator opened directly into the tracking room, which had crap piled to the ceiling.

Of course, I also loved being there because that was where

Brad lived. He had his own man cave in a dark, dingy room in the back that looked out onto a decrepit alley. Next to his futon was a jar of coins and a pot pipe. The bathroom was disgusting, with various old toothbrushes and containers of peroxide that Brad used to bleach his own hair. A set of shelves held books by Henry Miller and Nabokov and assorted volumes of American history, and there were piles of clothes in the corners. Man cave or not, I wanted in.

Trouble was that Brad also had a nice clean apartment in Park Slope with another woman. He told me that he wanted to leave her, that he liked me and he would tell her soon, but until he did, we couldn't sleep together. I was so gone, I accepted it all, even though I was never sure whether the story about the girlfriend in Park Slope was true. Brad always says he saved me, and I certainly wanted to be saved, but thinking back, I don't think anyone was saved.

Before the record was complete, we released a few of the songs on an EP I called *Bloody Mother Fucking Asshole*. Though the song was already a hit in my shows, "BMFA" almost didn't make it as a recording. To get it down, I had gone on my own to Allaire Studios, on a repurposed estate at the top of Mount Tonche near Woodstock, to do some solo recording. After several hours of practicing with the engineer in a gorgeous big room with windows looking out over the surrounding country-side, I was finally ready to record. Maybe he was tired or maybe it was just meant to be, but after I finished what I thought was a great take, the engineer confessed he hadn't pressed the Record button. I was furious—Allaire was expensive and I had already been there all day. I tried to remain calm, though, because I knew I needed his help on another take. I decided I would take a nap and told the engineer to do the same. We reconvened at one in the morning and got the song. A few months later, Brad added bass and it was done.

That song on that EP would finally solidify and launch my career. Fittingly, the break happened in the United Kingdom.

Eight

I HAVE SPENT A LOT OF time in the United Kingdom. My dad was something of an Anglophile and lived in London for long stretches of time, first in West Hampstead and then St. John's Wood. That was another place Rufus and I would fly to for visits when we were kids. We would go swimming in the pool in Swiss Cottage and take walks on Hampstead Heath, and Loudon took us to see Madame Tussauds, the Changing of the Guard, the Tower of London, and other touristy stuff like that. I sent back postcards to our mom of the Crown Jewels and punks with blue mohawks. I even loved the jet lag, because it made you want to go to sleep and when you woke up you got to have a full English breakfast.

In London, everything smelled a little musty and the bathrooms were freezing, with hot water you had to turn on. The place felt so different, but not really, it was just old-world—magical yet safe-seeming. The streets went in circles, making it impossible for you to know where you were at any time, and kids were allowed in pubs. Rufus and I would terrorize my dad's English girlfriends, who were either timid and embarrassed or self-righteously certain that they were the one for him.

But eventually my dad would always leave England, and the English roses, because he was quintessentially American and has never been able to stay in one place or with one woman.

Those visits, and the fun I'd had careening through those complicated London streets, created a strong new persona in me—the traveler at home in many places. Someone who was happy to live out of a bag, to catch the plane, train, or bus that would deliver her to the next place where she would sing for a crowd, no matter its size. The songs are the same, your clothes are the same, your tendencies are the same, but each little town, each city, each country has a feeling, a smell, a look that allows you to trade a little bit of your old self for something new. Hope is the eternal engine of the traveler. For me, singing is the greatest gift because it lets me move through time and space on some type of mission, searching for success or simply experience, for love or only a connection.

I also loved England because of Glastonbury. The first time I went to the big music festival there was in 2000. I was with Lily, my mom, and my aunt, who were scheduled to close the Sunday night on the acoustic stage. My friend Mercedes's US visa had run out, so she was back home. She'd been going to Glastonbury since she was seventeen and knew its ins and outs well; Mercedes's dad is a big-time entertainment lawyer, so she grew up surrounded by British rock stars. We got her tickets, too, so she could be our guide.

Glastonbury is one in a dozen festivals like it, a festival on steroids. There are always so many musicians playing that festival, and so many things going on simultaneously, it's like being in a sped-up, condensed version of everything that's simultaneously wrong and right about life. I love the way festivals like Glastonbury also encapsulate music as a social phenomenon, the most ancient of the arts and the most mythical, where the artists are briefly godlike, with thousands of people watching and applauding them. As a performer at Glastonbury, you want to leave your mark.

People go there for the music, yes, but they also go to party—to live in the (often) rainy outdoors for a few days in a setting where just about anything goes, including, and maybe especially, drugs. Like Burning Man and other festivals, Glastonbury gives anyone who likes to take drugs the green light. For that reason, not all my performances at Glastonbury have been stellar, but there were some good ones.

The festival is like a temporary city set up in a huge swath of fields not far from Stonehenge, in one of the most mystical parts of England. It's a pretty staggering sight to take in, a music festival hosting one hundred fifty thousand people over five days, rising out of the valley like it, too, is mythological. The grounds are crisscrossed by major thoroughfares and secondary paths; there are traffic jams and even what you'd call "neighborhoods." Some participants show up weeks in advance to build structures and stages, even rides. Most of the people who attend sleep in tents, though there are trailers and decked-out caravans; a lot of the bands stay in their tour buses, coming and going on show days. The number of performers is amazing, anyone from the crazily famous to the almost totally obscure.

That first time, Lily and I had been traveling with Kate

and Anna on their tour for *Matapédia*, drinking beer backstage between numbers and trying desperately and without much success to get into trouble. Mercedes knew a lot of people at the festival, and she introduced us to the Green Fields and Stone Circle neighborhoods, which were a distance from the main stages, designed for hippie families and the real weirdos, including the shit-disturbers known as the "travelers"—circus types who gate-crashed in order to shake things up a bit. As I mentioned, there were a lot of drugs around: MDMA and Ecstasy, ketamine, speed, meth, acid, mushrooms, and pot. Not to mention various weeds, roots, and leaves—people would basically just chew on the dirt in hopes it might alter their minds. In the early afternoon, Mercedes and a group of hilarious strangers picked Lily and me up near the acoustic stage and became our funky festival buddies for the next twenty-four hours.

After promising Kate and Anna that we'd be back a half hour before showtime, we set off. Someone produced a bag of what looked like sticky brown powder, and Lily and I dabbed our wet fingers in it. It was MDMA, I was told, and I think it was the first time I ever tried it. I had taken Ecstasy before, but this was a little different in its delivery system—oddly communal, with everyone's dirty little fingers dipping into the baggie, which also meant you could control the dose. Climbing the hill, we watched the sunset from the Stone Circle, over the heads and tent tops of the thousands and thousands of people living this alternate reality, all trying to have experiences they might not remember but that would mark them in ways both good and bad. The smoke from hundreds of little fires rose up around us; flags waved and the whole place seemed to vibrate. Nudity, sex, drugs, and music: exactly what a young person like me wanted from life.

By the time we got back to play with Kate and Anna, we were as high as kites. I had never played in that condition before, and I don't think I have since—I would never have the guts to do a show of my own high, since I need to talk to the audience and appear to be in control. But this show wasn't exactly hanging on my performance, and I have to tell you that it felt absolutely great, even life-changing, to play my "Year of the Dragon" with the McGarrigles and their great band, closing the festival on the acoustic stage in front of five thousand people. Kate and Anna weren't even mad at us, really, especially given that we didn't fuck up.

Afterward, we ran off with our motley crew to finish the festival, inviting ourselves to join various campfires, where we stared into the flames, leaning our tired heads on one another's shoulders.

When Mercedes had moved back to London, she got a council flat near Highgate. In the run-up to the release of the *Bloody Mother Fucking Asshole* EP, I would go over to the UK fairly often to play shows; my earlier EPs and my performances there had won me a small but devoted following. I would almost always stay with her. Up on a hill, her flat was the perfect place to return to for a bath and a cup of tea after a night out. It wasn't always tea, but Mercedes was never a big drinker; more than anything, her house was a place to recharge, which is something I usually needed to do. You wouldn't call it restful, though. Mercedes would wake up on the earlier side of things, roll herself a cigarette, pick up the phone, and resume yelling at her mother like we were still living at Phil's, traipsing around in her torn negligee. That, coupled with the hangover I might have, was enough to push me out of the house most mornings and down the hill to a coffee shop, especially since Mercedes never had any coffee on hand, only tea. She was still getting over her broken heart, and my relationship with Brad, I admit, was a permanent heartache, and we commiserated together about the happiness we would never achieve, not seeing how happy and even joyful we already were.

One particularly bright and uplifting day when she and I were sitting around smoking and complaining about how much any break in the arts world depended on luck, my cell phone rang. It was Martin Scorsese's people, inviting me to sing in the movie *The Aviator*. Now, it has to be said that I got the call because both Rufus and Loudon were doing the same thing—all of us in nightclub scenes at the Copacabana—and also because we knew the music supervisor. But that wasn't the point. It was the serendipity of it, like I was suddenly in an old movie where the obscure little song-and-dance girl gets her Broadway break. The Scorsese people told me they would fly me first-class to LA that evening. Mercedes shoved my clothes into my bag and ran me a bath as I paced up and down the tiny apartment in excitement. Every few seconds, she and I would jump up and down to cheer my good fortune. She said, "You see, it's possible!"

I did see that, maybe for the first time.

* * *

If Lenny Waronker was Rufus's big champion, Barbara Charone was mine. A former well-respected music journalist who wrote for every major music publication, Barbara is the top music publicist in the UK (and one of my favorite people on the planet). Her clients include Madonna, Christina Aguilera, Depeche Mode, Rod Stewart, Elvis Costello, Keith Richards, and…my brother. She arranged for me to do a showcase of sorts in a small basement venue in Notting Hill shortly after Brad and I had completed and sequenced all the songs for a full-length album. When I showed up to play, she had packed the room with journalists and record company people who were not as blasé when it came to me as their counterparts in the United States had been.

The first interest came from a young man, Sean Adams, who couldn't have been older than twenty-two at the time. Sean ran an online music magazine called *Drowned in Sound*. He had ambitions to be a label and had already put out a hit single called "I Predict a Riot" by the Kaiser Chiefs, and he was able to wrangle some money from one of his partners to bet on me. Fine, I'd take it. The music industry was in free fall, and I knew there was unlikely to be one big signing for lots of cash. In May 2005, with the help of my longtime lawyer Joe Serling, *Martha Wainwright* became Drowned in Sound's first full-length release. Rounder Records in the States, MapleMusic in Canada, Shock Records in Australia, and V2 for the rest of Europe also signed on, to make a patchwork of territories. All were good people, some better than others. I celebrated with

Brad and Nick Hill and all the musicians at Raoul's on Prince Street. I had just turned twenty-nine and was happy to be able to pick up the tab and also to be able to pay Brad for his work.

When we realized that Rounder Records was not going to spend any money on promotion in the United States, I focused instead on the UK and elsewhere. With the help of Barbara and the staff at the labels, I was able to get reviewed and noticed. (In time, the record would go gold in Canada, the UK, and Australia.) I was over a hump, and I was happy. I wasn't on the covers of *MOJO* or *NME*, but I was in those magazines, and sometimes my name was on the front somewhere. People wrote articles about me; for the most part, journalists had good things to say about my songs and my voice, and had a story to tell about where I came from. It sometimes annoyed me that every article was centered around my family, but it was also understandable, and I was used to that by now. I had eked my way into the spotlight, sort of like I had eked my way into this world.

With the record out, we embarked on a tour of England and Europe. Spike, our tour manager, was a little rough around the edges. He ran with a tough crowd, biker types who were heavily tattooed and definitely with some jail time among them, but he had a good heart, cared a lot about the music, and when it came to the sound each night was extremely attentive to my voice. For part of the tour, our walk-on music was Ian Dury's "Sex & Drugs & Rock & Roll," and Spike and the crew really looked the part with their bomber jackets and Docs, very English. The monitor guy was also a coke dealer, so the per diems were spent pretty fast; he made a lot of money on that tour. We partied a lot on the bus, and one night when we got real loose, I persuaded Spike to show us *all* his piercings. So we were pretty close. Brad wasn't crazy about Spike, but Spike made it clear he worked for me and he would defend me to anyone, which is what I needed.

Since I was the artist, the show had to be more about me and not so much about the musicians. Which was fine for most of the players most of the time, except when it wasn't. It was sometimes really confusing for Brad. All the other musicians were able to take their checks and go home at the end of the tour or back to their rooms at the end of the night, but Brad couldn't do that. We would lie in bed in our shared room and he would comment on what he felt was going wrong in my career and how I should do things differently. We had coproduced the record, and he and I had agonized for years over it, but now the spotlight was on me. I was the one who had written all the songs and I was the one who sang them. The reality was that I could perform them all without the band, as I had done for years.

Sometimes in interviews, I would try to make the musicians more of the story, talking about Brad especially, because he was hurt that he wasn't more present in the press. But journalists didn't bite when I described the role he played as producer. I felt torn because I was actually happy. I was doing some big TV shows, such as Jools Holland and Graham Norton, and I felt that I deserved all the attention. But it was hard to ignore the fact that Brad was angry that the power dynamic in our relationship had shifted.

When we were off the road, we lived in my apartment on South Ninth in Williamsburg. Brad had slowly and reluctantly moved some of his stuff in, but he still wasn't sure about what he wanted. He said it was out of his fear of commitment, but who knows? Things between us were complicated. We were very close but also had our own lives. I had many friends, some who fit with Brad and some who didn't. Sometimes when I was gone on tour without him, he would call or text incessantly to try to keep tabs on what I was up to. He could be jealous. But he was very secretive about his own life and spent a lot of time with people I didn't know.

We connected mainly through our work. I kept on introducing him to everyone I knew, and he began working with a lot of them. He was turning into a competent engineer, and he produced and traveled with artists like Teddy Thompson and his mother, Linda, Sean Lennon, and even Rufus.

I wanted to be happy in my personal life as well as in my career. I needed Brad. I loved him and regarded him as my confidant, and I think back then he loved me, too. But a part of him resented me. I disappointed him because he wanted me to be more successful, and sometimes he told me so. Other times he told me I was brilliant but that I was going about my career all wrong. He didn't like my managers, he didn't like the other musicians I played with, he didn't like the hotels we stayed in or the labels I was signed to. It was not what he was expecting.

I think he thought my first record would make me truly famous and would bring *us* more success.

I wish I could look back at those years with Brad without the deep sadness I feel now, on the other side of a doozy of a messy divorce. Everyone says time will help. I won't talk too much about it, because of the kids and because it's so hard to do, but I will try to hold on to some of the good stuff.

So what *can* I say? I thought it was love. I hope it was love. It felt like love in that it hurt so much. I remember passing my hands over every inch of his body so I could register it in my mind. I liked his clothes, I liked his badly cut and home-dyed hair, I liked his hairy chest. I had my eyes on him all the time, like I had had my eyes on the other men I had loved before him. Like them, Brad didn't look back at me as much. Is this a father issue? Maybe. It seems like a deep insecurity. I never felt worthy. But as time passed, I didn't try as hard or obsess as much about his love. When I started to gain recognition as an artist and other people praised me and I felt good about myself, Brad didn't have as much power over me.

Just a couple of months after my first record came out, I performed on the acoustic stage at Glastonbury to a full house of my own, and then also on the Other Stage, the festival's second largest. It was pretty thrilling for me. Before my set on that large stage, I remember squeezing into the designer dress I wore under an old tattered kimono and taking the time to do my makeup, something I would usually do quickly. I wasn't too nervous and walked out in front of the crowd with a giant smile on my face. I was in good voice and the musicians and I had played so many shows on the tour by then, we were a well-oiled machine. Afterward, I traded my high heels for wellies, put on a poncho, and wandered around with Mercedes in a drug-and-alcohol haze, laughing madly and going from fire to fire, meeting strange and crazy people. Tripping, laughing, loving being outside. I walked so many miles that by the next morning I could barely stand up, my legs hurt so much.

I might as well tell my other Glastonbury story of epic excess here, so you have the full measure of what the festival inspires in me (or used to, before I had kids and grew a little older).

A couple of years later, I was at the festival solo. The day began sensibly enough with me climbing out of my tent and eating breakfast, accompanied by a cup of tea and a beer to settle my nerves. My friend Tom Hall was posing that year as my tour manager in order to get into the festival, and he had heard that Ed Harcourt was around. Ed is a great singer-songwriter, a cross between Tom Waits and Johnny Rotten, who straddles the upright piano with a whiskey in one hand, then jumps from the piano to the drums to the guitar, all the while yelling out his poetic lyrics. With his tight vest and sideways smile, he seems to express all his inner sadness and frustration with the flexing of his tattooed muscles. Tom, on the other hand, is an aristocrat with a degree in English poetry, the kind of handsome charmer who seems to pop out of bed without a single hair out of place, who keeps the drinks coming, the humor going, and the experience magnificent. Some people could find him to be a snob, but if I could have spent the rest of my life punting along canals in Cambridge or taking long walks over the moors in wellies with a hunting dog and Tom by my side, I would have. I had crushes on both Tom and Ed, but they are really like my brothers.

Ed had just done a show at the Park Stage, and when Tom and I found him, he was in a real state. I doubt he had slept all night. Ed and I started huffing poppers and couldn't stop, and that was really the end of us. Neither one of us could move all that far from where we were standing because of the laughing fits the poppers caused. It wasn't even noon yet. I was supposed to play later that day with a collective known as Africa Express, a musical experiment made up of musicians from Africa and England who were attempting to cross the boundaries of the developing and first worlds through music. A confusing notion, but it's often hard to describe what we should let music simply do. Anyway, I was happy to be asked to be a part of it because it was put together by Damon Albarn, the lead singer of Blur, who had invited me to Mali on a musical exchange the year before.

But by the time Africa Express started, I was in no shape whatsoever to be singing in front of people. First of all, I had lost my voice entirely from talking and screaming and smoking and whatnot, and secondly, I was still feeling the effects of the whatnot. That's when Tom, my fake tour manager, approached the woman acting as Damon's tour manager (no stranger to drugs and alcohol herself) to tell her that I wasn't able to perform. "Martha has lost her voice," Tom went on, adding that "Martha needs rest." The woman pointed to the side of the stage, where I was dancing wildly atop a huge speaker. "*That* Martha?" she said.

"Yes," Tom said. "*That* Martha." He walked away sheepishly, leaving me with Ed and a couple of other hardcorers.

We started to roam like a pack of wolves, looking for trouble. We pillaged the dressing rooms—basically just tent cubicles. Ed, like the drunken sailor he resembles, started flipping over the couches and things, at one point grabbing a potted plant, placed there no doubt to create some modicum of nicety for some twitchy rock band, and swinging it around and around. Dirt flew everywhere. We, his followers, laughed and fell over, egging him on at the same time as trying to stop him. But not really, of course.

More poppers, and after every huff, another wave of madness would rise up and come crashing down, with predictably stupid results. At one especially mad moment, Pete Doherty, who had been in the English press nonstop the past year for dating Kate Moss, appeared in one of the dressing rooms, high on heroin and surrounded by all his druggy lackeys, and Ed lunged at him. Apparently, they were acquaintances. Ed clocked him in the face, and Pete, with surprising dexterity and aim, returned the favor. We finally managed to pull them apart before anyone got hurt. Ed disapproved of heroin, I guess. Later, I saw Ed and Pete hugging it out in a corner.

When the poppers were done, we ended up looking for Ed's wife, Gita, whom we found in a nearby tent, wearing shades, on mushrooms, looking beautiful, whereas I was falling apart. I needed some girl talk to counteract all that male energy.

After Gita and I spoke for a while, I realized I didn't feel too well and left her to head toward the backstage area where my fellow wolves and I had committed various crimes throughout the evening and into the night, and where I knew there were actual toilets. It was 4 or 5 a.m. by then, and in the bathroom I startled a well-known model, who was with an assistant, trying to do a line in one of the stalls. Unlike everybody else at Glastonbury, I guess she needed to hide what she was doing. (It reminds me of the time I startled Madonna in the bathroom at a rehearsal space as she and the wardrobe person were desperately trying to squeeze her into her costume. Famous people don't like to be caught off guard.)

I left her to it and climbed into the scaffolding under the stage. Over the ringing in my ears, I could hear distant dance music and an occasional wave of people screaming in reaction to what they were hearing. All of them on a lot of drugs. I spat up, trying to feel better, but there was nothing in my stomach, so I did not feel much relief. It had been fun, until I had gone too far. Ed and Gita and Tom found me, and we retrieved my guitar and got the fuck out of there.

It had been a famously muddy Glastonbury, and when we made it to our van, I wrestled my muddy boots off and let them fall out the door as the van started moving. Ed had a few mushrooms left, which we nibbled as we watched the stars begin to fade out the van windows. On our three-hour drive back to London, we didn't listen to music or even talk. We rode in silence, passing Stonehenge as the sun rose and the real world came into focus around us.

Nine

I'VE MENTIONED THE TENSION THAT existed between my dad and me, and the way I always felt judged by him. Though it makes me ashamed, I feel I should say a little more about the complicated ways in which I also felt judged and dismissed by my mother.

I was performing at the Bloomsbury Theatre, on the campus of University College London, sometime after my record came out, and Kate and Anna happened to be traveling through the city on their own tour. I invited them to sit in, and also invited some friends along as guest performers. For some reason, I always feel the need to share the stage and make more work for myself. Maybe I think I can steal the show by outshining others, though that strategy hasn't worked yet because I always get really great people.

That night in London, we had my mom and my aunt, as well as Chris Stills, Ed Harcourt, Teddy Thompson, Thea Gilmore, and Beth Orton. (I can't remember if Beth made it to the stage. There were some tears and drama beforehand, and I had to quickly put it all out of my mind to concentrate on hosting the show.) Ed did two new songs, "Lachrimosity," a word he said he'd made up but that already existed, and "You Only Call Me When You're Drunk," which were highlights of the night, but which also perhaps set the tone for the rest of the evening.

I started drinking at the action-packed sound check, where we frantically rehearsed the guests' songs and put ourselves through our paces, stretching our musical abilities to their limits. I guess that's really why I've always liked these kinds of shows. You feel so alive and vital, like you've stepped into an old Mickey Rooney and Judy Garland movie in which the kids all get together to put on a show. Not that this should make you feel particularly vital because both of them are dead, but when you're a performer, you want to think you are as great as the greats. Anyway, Ed smashed away at the piano, Teddy played the guitar with such ease it seemed to be playing itself, and we singers swooped up as high as we could go and dipped down into our lower registers to find something beautiful. The best of us all, of course, was my mother, moving freely from instrument to instrument, smiling and cracking jokes, charming everyone and enjoying every minute.

Showtime arrived, and the mood was so good we paid no attention to the opening act, who showed up with a B3 organ along with a Leslie and was personally attended by three "staff," even though he was only about nineteen. It turns out he was an artist named James Morrison, who was being groomed by his label and management. He became pretty successful, but I try to not pay too much attention to those kinds of things. But my people and I were flying solo that night—solo of record companies, staff, money, and grooming.

I tried to cover up the rough edges by putting on some makeup. Before going on, I also liked to give myself a little pep talk in the mirror, although with my mother around, I didn't need to psych myself up as much, since she did it for me. The show went off without a hitch.

Pumped and excited, we all went back to the management company flat where I was staying, a nice place in Mayfair, with twenty-two-foot-high ceilings, a working fireplace, and French doors. (The management company, doing okay, wanted to look as though they were doing really well.) I was feeling good. Knowing who was involved, my tour manager had arranged for copious amounts of alcohol, and my funky London friends joined us, wearing all their great outfits, including hats, feathers, old fur coats, and vintage leather boots. Earlier in the day, I had bought a selection of stinky cheeses from a good cheese shop, and someone had cut some flowers from their garden and brought them to the gig as an offering to me, and they were on the table. It was almost civilized.

We all got shit-faced as usual—we're musicians, after all. And pretty quickly a darker tone set in. Soon, I was in tears about my career, my insecurity always a bottomless pit. And my mom piled on, telling me I was the definition of mediocrity, and that I'd never achieve excellence because I had no real interests. About then, the last stragglers sensed it was time to leave.

How did things escalate so fast and go so far? Booze, I know, but what was in us that the booze brought out? When she said I had no interests, and that my mediocrity was all my fault, I couldn't control myself. I did try to move away from her, but she followed me into the bedroom, still talking, and I went crazy. I saw red. So I pushed her down. No, I grabbed her by the arms and threw her down. I've never been so haunted as the moment I saw her hit the ground and look back up at me in fear. Thank god I didn't kick her.

She was right. I did lack interests. I worried that I would never be as good as she was, or Rufus, or anyone, really. But I was shocked when she said it, and it hurt. Kate was always about to get under people's skin and sometimes it drove people to react violently or to fear her. Even me. Especially me.

But now we were both shocked and we knew it had gone too far. We shared a cigarette in silence, drank some water, and got into our respective beds before the sun came up. The following morning was beautiful, and I slunk into her room with my head down. I climbed in next to her, and we said nothing, just cried together, looking out the floor-to-ceiling window onto a court-yard. We both apologized tenderly and quietly, but effusively, and then we put it behind us. We wanted to forget.

We also didn't want to leave each other just yet, so she accompanied me to my next gig in Bristol. That night, she and I played together to a full house in a Bristol church, and the music we shared saved our souls and washed away some of the guilt we both felt. It was a good night, and afterward, Kate and I sat outside under the stars for a long time, saying very little and wiping away tears.

In 2004, Kate started having attacks every few months, always at night. They were dramatic, with a lot of vomiting—to the point of throwing up a foamy froth—and sharp, stabbing pains in her abdomen. By then, she had been living on her own for a while in the building on Querbes. She was set in a solitary evening routine of snacking in front of the TV and, at first, she blamed the attacks on this bad habit. She was in her late fifties and had always been pretty healthy, almost never needing to go to a doctor; she didn't believe in checkups, mammograms, bone density monitoring, or any of the rest of the tests women her age treat as facts of life. She finally sought medical help in 2005, going to several doctors and specialists, accompanied by Anna. (I think it's important to underline the companionship she had with her sister. Her whole life, really, but especially during these last years.) The doctors were puzzled and threw around various theories and possible diagnoses, like Crohn's disease, as the attacks grew worse. No one ever mentioned cancer.

Australia is a place that I visit often, and it has always seemed magical to me, with its strange, prehistoric-looking animals and reversed sky. One time, my band and I got lost in Wombat State Forest and we tried to get our bearings from the stars. We laughed and laughed as we attempted to piece together any semblance of knowledge of the constellations of the Southern Hemisphere. I felt lucky to be there, lost in the forest of wombats.

But the first time I went there, in January 2005, my mom was already mortally ill and we didn't know it. That Australian trip would mark the beginning of her torturous road, during which she graced as many stages as she could in as many countries as she could, saying goodbye to her life as an artist and, in her way, passing the baton to me, urging me to take more and more space onstage and in life.

We flew, along with Anna and Rufus, the day after one of my mom's abdominal pain attacks. Kate wasn't sure whether or not she should travel, but she got on the long flight, had a few drinks, charmed people, and made no complaints, like a true stoic. We were all relieved to take a break from the Montreal winter. (The city can be so extremely cold in the winter that the commitment to live there is really a commitment.)

We were headed to perform at a Leonard Cohen tribute at the Sydney Opera House, which was going to be filmed for a documentary on his career called *Leonard Cohen: I'm Your Man*. Hal Willner produced the concert, and the guests included Beth Orton, Nick Cave, Jarvis Cocker, the Handsome Family, and Leonard's backup singers, Julie Christensen and Perla Batalla. Linda and Teddy Thompson were there, too, as well as Antony (now known as Anohni). Between Nick, Jarvis, and Teddy, all the women in the cast were pretty much swooning all the time. If Rufus had been straight, that would have put the girls over the edge.

I sang on "There Is a War." I remember once asking his daughter, Lorca Cohen, which of her dad's songs was her favorite, and that was her answer. I was a little surprised, but if you knew how conflicted and restless Lorca is, you would understand her reasons. (Lorca and I used to be good friends, but no more. Cross her and there is no coming back from it. If I were to paint her portrait, there would be a wide and deep backdrop of burned and still-burning bridges.) The concert and following film and soundtrack album contributed to Cohen's massive comeback, priming the world for his incredible return to touring (which was necessary, too, after he was left almost penniless by a former manager's theft and fraud). I also got to sing "Tower of Song" (in the movie, they annoyingly recorded U2 doing it separately and used that) and "The Traitor." Here I was, singing Leonard Cohen songs at the Sydney Opera House, when fifteen or so years earlier I had been carrying my blue boom box with his tape in it everywhere I went. Some dreams do come true.

A few years later, I actually had a chance to audition to sing backup for Leonard on one of those world tours. Leonard knew my music and was very supportive of me, having come to see me play a few times in LA. He had always given me good advice, like "Never listen to the label executives." One time, after hearing me practicing in Lorca's house, he told me I had something special. I was flabbergasted. In those days, I always stayed with Lorca when I came to LA to work or visit Rufus. Leonard lived upstairs and he was around a lot. Once, I saw him in the backyard in his fedora with a bowl of fruit neatly placed on a simple wooden chair beside him, a beautiful naked woman reclining on the edge of the hot tub nearby—as if every scene of his life was a photograph or a painting.

In the end, I decided not to take the job, even though it would have been an amazing gig. From what I understand, Leonard paid well and always took great care of his musicians and his singers and his crew. But there is only so much hip-swaying, oohing, and aahing I can do while clad in a black suit before I start feeling underused. (I still know *all* the parts, though, having once sung them so obsessively.)

After the tribute was over, Kate, Anna, Rufus, and I stayed on to do a small tour together—nepotism at its best. I hadn't released my first record yet and was the furthest thing from famous, but I was able to play my songs in front of the large and faithful Australian audiences who had taken Kate and Anna into their warm embrace decades earlier. It was the beginning of my relationship with the country and continent that would become one of my "best markets," but more than that, Australia became meaningful to me for the friends I made and for the opportunity to experience its sheer beauty.

Later in 2005, one of Kate's scans showed a mysterious blurry mark. Exploratory surgery was the only way to really find out what it was. The surgeon, Dr. Tabah, explained that the blurry bit could be something inconsequential, like scar tissue left from the severe bout of peritonitis Kate had barely survived in her twenties (more about that later), but he thought it was wise to check it out.

Looking back, I think we were already dancing around the truth. It wasn't scar tissue. Kate was recovering from the surgery when Dr. Tabah came in to tell us that he had discovered a large tumor in her upper colon that had almost completely obstructed her digestive tract. It was about the size of a fist, big and nasty, and if he hadn't removed the thing, she could have died from the obstruction. He'd removed the surrounding lymph nodes, too, and had also caught sight of a few small lesions on her liver. He looked particularly concerned when he

My aunt Teddy and Kate at a motel, somewhere in time. Kate is pregnant with Rufus. *Martha Wainwright Collection*

Rufus, me, and my grandmother, Martha, taken in New York by my grandfather, Christmas, 1977. *Loudon Wainwright, Jr.*

Family on ice. *(Left to right)* Sylvan, Anna, Rufus, Kate, and me, taken by Randi Saharuni in Venise-en-Quebec, 1980.

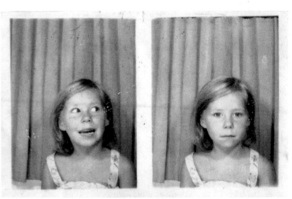

Happy/sad, my two faces in a photo booth in Montreal, circa 1981. *Martha Wainwright Collection*

Me and Rufus and Jesse Radz singing "Dead Skunk" at my dad's show, London, circa 1984. *Martha Wainwright Collection*

Me, Sylvan, Rufus, and Lily, St. Raphael's Ruins, Ontario, 1984. *Dane Lanken*

(Left to right) Dane Lanken (Anna's husband), Rufus, Sylvan, Lily, me, and photographer David Gahr at the Newport Folk Festival, perhaps singing a Stephen Foster song. *Martha Wainwright Collection*

Rufus and me in 1980, probably visiting Dad in Waccabuc, New York. *Martha Wainwright Collection*

Rufus and me making a birthday tape singing "Happy Birthday" for our grandmother. Shelter Island, summertime, circa 1987. *Loudon Wainwright*

Me around age eleven, wearing my typical happy face and feeling dubious of the world, at our house in Saint-Sauveur. *Martha Wainwright Collection*

My grandmother Gaby, Lily, and me at the house in Saint-Sauveur, circa 1989. *Martha Wainwright Collection*

My tenth-grade photo when I returned from my difficult year living with Loudon, became a separatist, and started doing theater, 1991. *Martha Wainwright Collection*

Me with Ariel Engle, who would later join Broken Social Scene, at my apartment on Querbes, when we were both about seventeen years old, circa 1993. *Martha Wainwright Collection*

Me in Tokyo during that first, fateful trip to Japan in the nineties as Rufus's back-up singer. I found this old guitar on the street in this alley. *Martha Wainwright Collection*

Sad limo times. Rufus and me singing and smoking in the nineties. *Martha Wainwright Collection*

Me feeling a little sad in Montreal, circa 1997. *Martha Wainwright Collection*

With my friend and advocate Nick Hill in New York, circa 1999. *Martha Wainwright Collection*

Me and my roommate Phil Marshall, probably after one of our many late nights spent philosophizing, by the East River on the Williamsburg, Brooklyn waterfront, circa 1999. *Mercedes Grower*

Gavin Friday, Lou Reed, Rufus, and Van Dyke Parks at Hal Willner's Harry Smith tribute concert, which took place at St. Ann's Church in Brooklyn, New York, on November 12, 1999. *Martha Wainwright Collection*

Me and Rufus at Pierre Marchand's studio while Rufus was making *Poses* in 2000. *Pierre Marchand*

Backstage in Wolverhampton, circa 2000, with Lily and Kate in the background. *Jeff Hill*

The wedding singers who serenaded me as I walked down the aisle on September 2, 2007: *(Left to right)* Joel Zifkin, Chaim Tannenbaum, Kate, Dane, Lily, Anna. *Martha Wainwright Collection*

With my mom, Kate, at Drury Lane in London, when I was performing in *Seven Deadly Sins* at Covent Garden in 2009. *Martha Wainwright Collection*

Me, Rufus, and Kate at the premiere of Rufus's opera *Prima Donna* in Marsden, UK, on July 10, 2009. I'm a few months pregnant and Kate is ill. *Bernadette Colomine*

My mom and me on my trip to say goodbye, a few moments before I returned to England on December 27, 2009. *Lily Lanken*

My dad, Loudon, and his grandson, my son Francis, at our house in Brooklyn in 2014. *Martha Wainwright Collection*

Arc and Francis in Montreal's Chinatown in November 2016. *Martha Wainwright Collection*

Playing in 2021. *Camilla Lundbye*

mentioned those. Dr. Tabah was kind but clear: the lab would need to biopsy the tumor to make absolutely sure of what it was, but he doubted it was benign. In fact, he used the opposite word: *malignant*. And the lesions on her liver indicated that the cancer had probably spread.

A day later, Kate was moved to a large, bright, single-occupancy room, which Dr. Tabah had pulled strings to get for her. We all gathered around, each with our different reactions to the news. Anna got on the computer and started doing research on possible treatments. Aunt Jane—who had looked so calm while the doctor was telling us the results of the surgery, it was as if she hadn't even heard him—retreated for a while, and Rufus kept himself really busy with work. Since there was room for a cot beside Kate's bed, I packed my pajamas and toothbrush and moved in for the next few days.

On that first night I spent sleeping in Kate's room, everything changed between us. I never questioned her or raised my voice to her again. Whatever difficult mother-daughter dynamic we had had in the past vanished. I was very teary and spent more time than I probably had to in the hospital-room bathroom crying. Brad, I remember, found me there, and took me by the shoulders and kissed me very hard.

The last time I'd been in a Montreal hospital, I was eighteen and there to have an abortion. After looking through a phone book to try to figure out how to get one, I finally broke down and asked my mom for help. She told me to call the hospital to make an appointment, which I did. She also spoke to our family doctor, who had taken such good care of my grandmother. He's one of those doctors with a soothing voice and soft cool hands that make you feel better all on their own. He'd come to the house in Saint-Sauveur when my grandmother died. Her body lay in the small downstairs bedroom where she had spent the last few months of her life because she was too frail to get up the stairs. He was a spiritual man, the follower of an Indian guru, and he was also the guru's doctor; he'd brought him to a mountain to die. Though Gaby was already gone, he'd rubbed her forehead with his thumb to help "release her soul," as he said. The gesture seemed very kind.

After my mom had filled him in, he asked me to come see him. At our appointment, he made it clear that whatever I did in response to the pregnancy was fine with him, but he recommended that if I went through with the abortion, it might help for me to take a moment, if it felt right, to say goodbye to the child who wouldn't be, through a dedication or prayer or something of the sort. On my ride home from his office, on the 24 bus along Sherbrooke Street, I apologized and tried in some way to set us both free. When I got home, Anna was there with Kate and they told me that if I wanted to keep the baby, they would take care of us both. I thanked them but told them that I wasn't ready to be a mother. I'm sure they were relieved, but a little sad, too. The next day, my mom drove me and my boyfriend to the hospital and waited for us outside.

Now, years later, I wheeled Kate out to that parking lot after she was released, as I would over and over again during her illness, always hoping not to have to return, and always knowing we'd be back.

Ten

By this time, Brad and I had been together for five years. Even though our relationship was tricky, I wanted to marry him. I thought it would bring both of us some much-needed stability and set us on a path for a family. I guess I also wanted to grow up before my mother died. She wanted so badly to see me happy.

The truth is, Brad needed to grow up, too. The touring and our home life in New York were equally unsettled, as well as muddled with drugs and alcohol. The thing about being an artist or a musician is that there is very little certainty; you don't know whether you'll be able to earn a living or not, whether anyone will come out to hear you or not. On the personal front, I felt like every time Brad and I fought, there was the risk that we would break up. With my mother's diagnosis, the demands of my career, and the less-than-calm relationship I had with Brad, I felt we needed a change that would make our lives more positive, sustainable, and stable. A marriage? Perhaps it sounds crazy, given what I've said about Brad so far, but it wasn't really. I was thirty at the time, and I wanted to be like my aunt Anna and her husband of forty years, Dane, or like Nick and Alex. Most of all, I wanted to have children.

So I put pressure on Brad to get married, though I found out he was going to propose before it happened. While I had some great moments with Brad, this wasn't one of them. He had gone on the road with Sean Lennon and was in Europe or someplace else far away. Lily and I were hanging out at my apartment in Williamsburg. We'd gone barhopping and by the time we got back home, we were pretty lit up. Both of us wanted a little bump. I knew Brad always had some coke hidden in the apartment. (I would find out later, Brad hid a lot more than his coke from me. We were so different in that way. I always wore everything on my sleeve and Brad always kept his hand hidden.) When I called him to ask where the drugs were, he got mad and started chewing me out for partying. He often got mad if I hung out with other people when he wasn't around, which felt strangely possessive, but he always billed it as being concerned for me. I argued back, and when he finally gave in, he warned me that I would also find something else. "Maybe I'm making a mistake," he said.

When I asked him what he meant, he merely directed me over the phone to the back of his top drawer where I located the stash, but also a receipt from Tiffany's for a lot of money. He said, "Now you know. I was going to ask you to marry me but you've ruined it." I was surprised, and sad—I never would have noticed the receipt if he hadn't said anything—but also sort of happy. When he got back, we didn't speak about it.

A few weeks later, we headed for St. Sauveur to celebrate Christmas with my family. On Christmas morning, we were having coffee in one of the four little cabins on the property, sun streaming in the window, happy with each other for once, and Brad presented me with a beautiful engagement ring and asked me to marry him. I never expected a ring. No one I knew had ever had a ring. But that's the way they did things in Brad's family, and he wanted to do this right, I guess.

Kate was on the phone in the kitchen of the big house when I ran in to tell her the news. I can still see her, holding on to the weighty receiver of the old black rotary phone connected to the wall by maybe two feet of hardened coiled line. When I beamed at her and flashed my ring finger, she said, "You're the first person in this family to have a diamond." That was about it. I think she was annoyed that we had decided to do this, though over the course of the day, she grew more encouraging.

I soon found out that she had known for months Brad was going to propose, because he had asked both her and my brother for their consent. Apparently, they both asked him if he was certain marriage was a good idea. Writing this now, it seems like our marriage was doomed from the start. But I don't regret it. I don't regret it at all. I was deeply in love with him and we did fit together, at least for a time. Our children are the testament to that and the gift that came out of our turbulent and imperfect relationship.

Brad and I were now so intertwined that I thought it would be best to make my second record with somebody else. I'd gotten used to playing with a band and, as a result, some of the songs I was writing were a little more rocky and upbeat than the stuff on my debut album. In classic form, the labels and I felt that my second record could afford to be more pop and commercial, a pretty common trajectory for singer-songwriters. I had gotten a taste of the limelight and wanted to be more famous (maybe not as famous as Brad wished I was) and to make more money.

Well, the fame and money haven't come through yet, but I have to say I really like the second record, though it didn't turn out to be poppy in the slightest. It does succeed at being aggressive, which is maybe not the most attractive trait in my music, but at least it's refreshing to hear a woman who is not the least demure or coquettish.

In the end, Brad ended up producing some songs on the album, basically because he didn't like what the other producers were doing. I had been doing a lot of shows in Norway and Sweden and worked with two different producers from there, Martin Terefe (KT Tunstall, Jason Mraz, James Morrison) and Tore Johansson (Franz Ferdinand, the Cardigans, OK Go), who are career pop producers with credits that go on and on forever. Brad felt he needed to step in and fix things. I felt I needed to let him produce some songs so he'd be happier. Maybe we accomplished both? I don't know. We were all tangled up in blues.

The title of the record became *I Know You're Married but I've Got Feelings Too*, a line from one of the songs, "Bleeding All Over You." (Brad didn't much like the title either.) On it, there are songs about restlessness and about wanting to be loved, about my tormented love for Brad, about my friend George dying, about wishing I were someone else, and risqué lines about "my hole." There are two relatively unfriendly songs about Loudon, so I think he and I are even on that score. There's also one about Kate's cancer. I called it my "Scandinavian" record.

Both Donald Fagen and Pete Townshend played on it. I met Pete and his partner, Rachel Fuller, when they had invited me to appear on their online TV show and Pete played along on a couple of my songs. I was overwhelmed, but it was the beginning of a friendship with the innovative and brilliant artist and his wonderful partner. These musical relationships with my elders (fathers?) have always been important to me. Rufus, Lily, and Kate are also on the album. We recorded tracks in London, Malmö, Sweden, and New York, perfect for the traveler in me.

When I go back and listen to these older records, I regret that most people will never hear them or know anything about me and my work. There are a ton of artists in the world who live in near obscurity when all they want is to be heard. That was true then and it is still the case, no matter the stories about people breaking out by way of videos made in their bedrooms and shared on YouTube or Instagram or TikTok. (I'm really bad at social media, partially because of my age but also because my platform has always been a stage or the studio.) Now that I run a music venue in Montreal, I'm solicited all the time by people who want to play there. Nothing has changed, though. They can drop a cassette tape in the mailbox or send me their Bandcamp—it doesn't really make a difference (although the cassette would be more fun).

Making a record in those days was the culmination of years of work—writing the songs, rewriting the songs, playing them in public, and then recording them, sometimes over and over again. It cost thousands upon thousands of dollars and took days and weeks and months of time, and everyone gave so much of themselves, and then we put it out there and hoped it got noticed and sold millions of copies and won a Grammy and ended up as the soundtrack of a big ad or in a movie. In my case, it is so unlikely, and yet I keep doing it. It almost makes me want to cry. In so many ways, my career is a failure, but it feels so good to make music, and play with other people, and fill the room with my own sound, and have the words I've written be heard. It's an addiction, I guess, like any other.

Our wedding, which took place over the Labor Day weekend in 2007, was one for the books. My mother and I spent months organizing it. The angry daughter was gone, and I tried to be the good daughter, a role I wish I'd taken on years earlier. I wasted so much time fighting with my mom, and I regret it terribly. But there's not much I can do about it, other than remember the good things and the best times.

The hours we committed to creating a magical wedding were one of the best times. We both knew how to throw a party, and I wanted this one to be hers as much as mine. With our relatives and her friends and mine, we ended up with a guest list of around two hundred people. Anna, who prefers small, understated affairs, thought the entire thing was silly, and even frivolous. Why did I insist on such a big wedding, she wanted to know, and why did it have to be at St. Sauveur?

I reminded her that the last time our extended family and friends had come together was for Gaby's eighty-fifth birthday, two decades earlier. Our family needed a great big gathering and celebration. We could invite all the beloved stragglers, including all my mother's and aunt's cousins who lived in the area; all of Kate's closest friends just happened to be Anna's friends, too. Then there was everyone who mattered to me: Friends from London like Mercedes and Barbara, Tom, and Ed. Friends from LA like Lorca Cohen, Leonard's daughter. The New Yorkers, especially Nick and his family, and Phil. All the Montreal crew from my childhood and adolescence. Brad's family. Basically, it would be like a big dream (nightmare?) in which all our worlds collided. And everyone would play: my dad, Brad's dad, Emmylou Harris, Linda Thompson, my half sister Lucy, Mom and Anna, Rufus...

I took Lorca with me to Paris to buy my wedding dress. Lorca had lived there with her mom, Suzanne (not the namesake of the song, something that she must have had to explain a thousand times). Like both her parents, she likes pretty things and is very opinionated about style. Who better to help me find a dress?

The two of us went to Le Bon Marché, on Paris's Rive Gauche, and made a beeline for the gown department. I knew I didn't want a traditional wedding dress, but I did want something formal, so we browsed the kind of stuff you wear to the

Oscars or to balls, if you do that kind of thing. I settled on an off-white dress covered with galloping mauve horses in a 1940s V-shape style, with ruching in the front, shoulder pads, and a small train I later had to cut off so I could cut up on the dance floor. I still have that dress in the feckless hope I might be able to do something creative with it one day. Maybe it can be my shroud. (I save a lot of things like this because I continue to wish I were someone who makes her own clothes and does a lot of crafts. More likely, the moths will get it before I ever transform it.)

A few weeks before the wedding, I was in Europe, playing a bunch of shows. I flew back to New York from Amsterdam, exhausted and depleted, no doubt the result of a certain amount of debauchery mixed with the hard work on my part. Brad was out of town, and I didn't want to be alone that night, so after I landed, I arranged to go for dinner with Reuben, a very good friend from the neighborhood. After we'd eaten and drunk a lot of wine, Reuben pulled out all these mushrooms he'd accumulated over the years and stored in his freezer, and we made a pot of mushroom tea and drank it.

An hour later, we were both feeling and acting pretty silly. We felt it might be dangerous to go out into the streets, so we stayed in his dingy and depressing living room for what seemed like months. His girlfriend, Johanna, who hadn't partaken in this psychedelic fun, got fed up with us and went to bed, leaving Reuben and me to play the guitar, run our fingers over each other's forearms as lightly and delicately as we could (I did have to remove Reuben's hands from my ass several times in a male-female best friend kind of way), surf the TV in search of what we could mutually agree were the funniest things in the world (commercials mostly), and listen to our own music along with songs by other people we liked— Yo La Tengo, Sonic Youth, and Neil Young, as I recall.

By the time the sun was about to come up, I needed to sleep. My stomach was upset, too, from the mushrooms, the jet lag, and all the cigarettes I'd smoked. I told Reuben to go to bed, and I lay down on the couch with a sheet over me. An hour or two later, I woke up with stomach pains and dashed to the bathroom. I splashed some water on my face and took off all my clothes, I was so hot, but I still felt queasy and sweaty, and my head was spinning. I took a seat on the toilet and placed my head in my hands to try to calm my body and brain. I closed my eyes, and the next thing that happened is something I hope never to experience again. When I slowly opened my eyes, a cat was staring at me from a few feet away, backlit in bright sunlight. I was lying in the hall, with my head resting in a sticky pool of blood. I'd passed out, it seems. The bathroom was small, and I must have hit my head on the sink before toppling off the toilet and into the hallway. I have no idea how long I was out for, but the blood had already coagulated. Thank god it was the cat that found me, and no one else, but even so, I was completely ashamed in front of this creature. As I wobbled to my feet, the cat put out its tongue and took a little experimental lick of the blood on the floor. When I turned around to look in the mirror, I discovered that I had gashed open one of my eyebrows and there was blood running down the side of my face.

I kicked my underpants off and got into the shower, letting the water flow over me, cool first and then warmer. I started to cry a little since I still felt like shit. When I got out, I wrapped myself up in a towel and pressed a bunch of wet paper towels against the gash to stanch the bleeding. Then I lay down on the couch again in the hope of getting some sleep, but when I checked the paper towel a minute later, it was saturated. The cut wouldn't stop bleeding.

I was scared enough to call Brad in Europe. He calmed me down, telling me I would be all right. I would feel normal in a day or so. Something like this would never happen again. We all make mistakes. I was just exhausted from all the traveling and touring. There was a lot going on. The wedding. The new record. Kate's cancer. He was helpful.

The blood eventually stopped pouring out of my eyebrow. I cleaned up all the mess; only the cat had to witness the worst of that. I'm not an animal person, but I liked that cat from then on. I felt we had been through something together. When Reuben and Johanna got up, I told them I needed to get some stitches, but not before we all went out for a Mexican breakfast. We were all starving. Johanna lent me a new shirt and a pair of sunglasses so I could face the world.

Afterward, Reuben drove me to Beth Israel hospital. I didn't have health insurance, and when the nurse finally saw me, I confessed everything—that I had smoked pot and drunk wine and taken mushrooms and fallen over after getting off a plane from Amsterdam. Like a true emergency room nurse, she didn't bat an eyelid. She gave me six neat stitches just above my eyebrow that were programmed to dissolve within a week and leave almost no scar. The only problem, she said, was that I would have a black eye for a month or two.

It wouldn't be a great look, especially for a wedding. But the show had to go on.

The wedding weekend was perfect. The day before the ceremony, Rufus organized a party a few miles up the road at a beautiful, dilapidated, and rambling lake house owned by Susanne Bartsch, the New York club and fashion icon and party organizer. His band, complete with a four-piece horn section, played Italian wedding songs in honor of Brad and his family.

The guests stayed at the few motels peppered around town, all of which were within walking distance of the property, including the old, slightly run-down Motel des Pentes, which turned into the home base for the most rockin' set of people. A friend of mine mistook the name for Spanish, and from then on, we all called it "Motel des Pentez" as if we were in Mexico. Jimmy Fallon stayed there and held court, though as I was busy getting ready to be a gracious hostess, I never got to see him in action. People told me he spent the mornings cracking jokes by the side of the miniature motel pool, wearing a silly, tiny Speedo, a cocktail in his hand. He was being groomed for his talk-show host job at the time. We met through a mutual friend in the theater world and had immediately gotten very close. I must admit we had a thing for one another. Or maybe it was just me who had the thing, but he was pretty convincing.

My dad had chipped in a little to cover the cost of this extravaganza, and Brad and I put in what we could, too, but I later found out that Kate had taken out a bank loan in order to pay the rest and was so scrupulous she had gotten life (or death?) insurance on the loan. She knew she wasn't going to make it much longer and that, this way, the loan would be wiped. It was sad, but smart.

Kate and Anna and Dane, Lily, Sylvan, and Chaim Tannenbaum, an old friend of both my mom and my dad, sang folk songs while people arrived, and Tom Mennier wrote a piece he called the "St. Sauveur Waltz" that danced me down the aisle. My father held my arm. We said our vows under the pine trees. I remember Brad's tense expression and his clenched jaw; he seemed afraid. I was goofy and felt like I was on display in a way I didn't like. I don't know if other people getting married love that moment of saying yes. I imagine some do, but it was hard for me, perhaps because it seemed to be a spectacle rather than an intimate moment between Brad and myself.

Still, there was a lot of joy, a lot of music, and the food was great. I had found a caterer in Montreal who made méchoui, a whole lamb roasted for hours on a spit. My mom and I had hand-picked all the cheeses and wines, and the sophisticated burnt sugar cake was a recipe she'd made for years. We had a huge tent, with a wood floor, that turned into a magical space. Nick was the master of ceremonies, and he got the ball rolling after the ceremony by inviting people up to serenade

Brad and me. First Loudon, then Emmylou, then Rufus, then Linda. Jimmy Fallon got the party to their feet by singing an incredible version of some Doors song with the band, made up of musicians who were there as guests. And then Brad's dad knocked us all out with his version of "A Nightingale Sang in Berkeley Square." It was very important for Brad and me to have all our parents there. Brad and I are both the products of divorce, brought up by our moms with only moderate contact with our dads, but fully influenced and affected by our fathers. It was very important to both of us to have all four of our parents there. My dad seemed a little nervous about it all, as usual, and I noticed that Brad's dad took him aside for what my dad thought would be a talk about the newlyweds but instead was a request for record label advice.

Two tables—table 8! table 9!—seemed to compete over the dinner hours for attention and ratings. They were filled with performers and extroverts: Justin Vivian Bond, Tom Hall, Jimmy, Barbara, Reuben, Ed Harcourt, and other people who liked to have a good time. A friend had brought along a lot of good blow as a wedding gift, and also paid for the minister, really covering all the bases.

By 2 a.m., when we lit bonfires, most of the guests were still there. The live music had wound down somewhat, and people had migrated to the fires, when they weren't getting up to do stuff in the shadows. During my welcoming speech, I had invited, even urged, everyone to join in the spirit of a wedding and have sex if they wanted. There is something about a fire outside in the night that loosens people's inhibitions, and some had taken me up on my invitation, having "quickies" in various corners of the property. Two hours later, at 4 a.m., half the guests were still there and Rufus was blaring opera out the living room windows.

Everyone was still happy. No one had gotten hurt. A few people had cried. My cousin's girlfriend had slept with one of the members of Rufus's band, and a few people had had too much to drink, but overall it was a good night. Anna had had a great time, dancing and staying up drinking until very late. Kate had put her illness to one side that night and was her old self, drinking champagne and staying up with Rufus in the living room, terrorizing people with her charm and her wit and her fiery beauty, singing and playing the piano, the guitar, and possibly the bass, while Anna joined in on guitar, accordion, and even the drums at one point.

I ended up going to bed in one of the little cabins at around six in the morning. Brad was still awake when the crew came to strike and drag away the wedding tent. My hangover the next day was bad, but worth it, too. A few hours later, I watched from a tiny window as people drove in to say goodbye before they headed back over the border or to the airport. It wasn't until four that afternoon that I could face another human being. The fires smoldered the whole day as a reminder that I was now married.

Why did I get married? Me, of all people. I got married because I loved Brad, but also because my mom was dying and I wanted to show her that I was going to be all right. I wanted to have a child for myself and also so that she could hold a grandchild before she died. I just wanted her to have everything life could offer. And I wanted that for me, too. Oh boy, did I get it. The good and the bad.

In the days leading up to the wedding, I'd had lots of second thoughts, but I was too afraid to back out. I admit that on the day of the service, while I was wrapping the long suede cords of my high-heeled shoes around my ankles (might as well have been my neck), I thought to myself, *I can always get divorced.*

Eleven

AFTER OUR WEDDING WAS OVER, my mom grew sicker. Before long, she was spending a lot of time in the hospital. The various surgeries are all a little blurry in my memory. Clearest in my mind is her first major operation, or at least flashes and images of it. Like the other members of my family in the hospital that night, I kept wondering whether it was all really happening. I also remember the overwhelming fear, and the strength of the love I felt for my mom, and the shock of seeing her afterward, intubated and connected to all sorts of drips and to a catheter, too. I had zero experience of this, but I would quickly learn the reasons for and the functions of the various tubes and attachments. What I didn't know at the time was it would only get worse.

Hospitals are strange. They house the best and worst of life. Birth and death, illness and recovery. A hospital is like a little terrible city of its own, and when you spend a lot of time there, you become part of it—saying hello to the nurses and the other staff, helping yourself to the linens in the closet, bringing in your own food, setting up your photos and your plants and your toiletries.

After her second big surgery, Kate was rolled into the ICU to find my cousin Lily and me there to greet her. The drugs they'd given her can make anybody pretty funny—laugh-funny, I mean—and I remember Kate asking Lily to take her picture and that she wanted to caption it "Me Tube."

Kate would get better and come home for a few months at a time. Depending on what treatment she was on, she had some energy. Other times, she would sink into the couch for days at a time.

Life had to go on and money had to be made. About a year after her first big surgery, Kate came to London to see me do a gig with the Royal Ballet at Covent Garden, singing along to Kurt Weill's *The Seven Deadly Sins*, since for some reason I had convinced myself I could sing Kurt Weill and be in the ballet. (Actually, Will Tuckett, the choreographer, was the one who invited me to do this production, and I'll always be very grateful to him for that.)

The score was hard to sing. It didn't have any of Weill's identifiable, hummable songs like "Mack the Knife" or "September Song," just tenuous melodies I had to sing in a difficult range because the Kurt Weill Foundation for Music does not allow performers to change any of the keys. I was blissfully out of place, a fish out of water taking deep breaths that were killing me to handle the phrasing, but I did as well as I could. After the show, I bowed and accepted the flowers that the company arranged to buy beforehand so as not to embarrass the performers who don't receive flowers from the uber ballet fans who show up at the stage door with giant bouquets for the prima ballerinas. Ballet fans are definitely weirder than rock fans.

I had taken ballet as a girl and was excited to be a part of it now as an adult. I felt like an impostor but also loved pretending to belong to the company. After I arrived in London, I went straight to a ballet shop and bought myself some ballet slippers and a few leotards. I joined the classes in the morning and would stand at the bar wedged between some of the most famous dancers in the world. I would watch their feet and stumble along as they went through their paces. I stretched till it hurt and awoke muscles that had been dormant for years. I walked around the halls with my toes pointed outward and my hair in a bun. I only nibbled on my food, kept my back straight while I was seated, and looked ridiculous (a little like that *French and Saunders* ballet dancer skit).

The Covent Garden performances happened to coincide with my mom's sixty-third birthday, and since she was staying with me and Brad in a big apartment the ballet had rented for me on Drury Lane, I'd planned a birthday celebration for her and invited a lot of people. Whether it was the excitement of the show, the weight of Kate's illness, or just my nature, I was feeling reckless. While there was no performance of *Seven Deadly Sins*, the ballet, on the night of Kate's birthday, there was a performance of *Seven Deadly Sins* by Martha Wainwright.

Kate's good friend Deborah, a former ballet dancer herself (she's on the cover of the McGarrigles' *Dancer with Bruised Knees*), had traveled from Montreal with Mom in order to help; after surgeries and chemotherapy, Kate was becoming more and more frail. One side effect of Kate's chemo was hand-foot syndrome, which meant the skin on her hands and feet had grown so sensitive she could hardly use them. They were peeling, too, so she had to put a salve on and wrap them in cloth bandages or wear white cotton gloves to protect them from cracking open. At its worst, she couldn't hold anything, or button up her pants, or walk for more than a couple of blocks.

Anyhow, despite all this, Kate was a sport as usual, helping me as much as she could as I made and served the food I'd bought at Borough Market that morning. When everything was ready, she allowed herself a couple of drinks, and the two of us played some music together in one corner of the living room. I had an electric guitar with a little amp, because I always thought I should play electric guitar—which I don't—and Kate strummed along on the acoustic. I was working on a song, and she helped me with some ideas, which she rarely did. (I have never succeeded in collaborating on or cowriting a song. I'm dreadfully private and very self-conscious about it and if someone overhears me or sees any lyrics before they are done, it makes me nervous.)

Friends from the ballet started arriving, the wine was flowing, and there was dancing. (Ballet dancers can be really bad at dancing to pop music, their gestures so over the top it makes them very funny to watch.) Kate danced a little, too, but she soon grew tired and headed off to bed. After the wave of guests left, Brad retired for the night, and then the late shift arrived—friends who liked to walk on the wild side from time to time. My good friend Tom came, along with his American roommate, who always had lots of drugs, and Tom's then girl-friend, "Alabama," as we called her, since that's where she came from. She was some kind of American heiress, and possibly worth billions, and Tom had swept her off her feet while she was going through a bad divorce. We proceeded to take MDMA, and as it started to kick in, the clothes started coming off. Tom slipped into one of my ballet leotards, and Alabama and I were down to our underwear, hers a thong as I recall, and mine not, and at any one point, two of the three of us had giant lampshades on our heads. I can't remember what we were dancing to, but the soundtrack certainly included Laurie Anderson's "O Superman," a song that's perfect for interpretive dance, one element we introduced being attempting a head-stand on the dining room table.

Brad, who wasn't that fond of my London friends, stumbled out of our room a couple of times to remind us that my sickly mother and her friend were trying to sleep. After his third or fourth attempt, my mom herself appeared in our midst in her nightclothes and white gloves, with an expression on her face that said, "Don't fuck with me, I'm dying." I briefly entertained the idea of taking the party to Tom's apartment, but Kate soon convinced Tom and Alabama and whoever else was on these crazy, stupid drugs to go home, and me to go to bed. The sun was about to come up, and she, Kate, had to leave for the airport in a few hours to fly home for more chemo.

I don't think she was mad at me, but I think she was worried. She knew she'd be leaving me for good soon, and here I was, still a mess. Also, this wasn't the first time I had done this to her while she was sick. There was also the time I was staying with her in Montreal when Chris Stills and his band came to town for a show. Kate's foot had a massive fucked-up sore on it, the result of wearing a pair of too-tight boots she'd laced up one day because she couldn't resist going for a last cross-country ski. All she had wanted was to be in the sunlit forest, breathing and moving in the cold air, doing something good for herself. But no, the boot rubbed a spot on her foot raw, and it became infected, her heel turning into a huge oozing mess. I was meant to be taking care of her, but I went to my friends' show instead, and afterward thought it was a good idea to bring them all home to say hi. Kate loved Chris and his bass player, and they were happy to see her, too, though I'm sure they were also surprised at the condition of her foot. After, I took them downstairs to my old ground-floor apartment to drink and do a lot of blow, and I'm sure we kept my mom up with loud music and even louder talking. Then Anna showed up to take Kate to the emergency room, as I was in no shape to go. The two of them waited there for hours while my friends and I carried on, blabbing our heads off. Later, I went to see Kate in the hospital. That time she looked mad, though she didn't say anything other than to tell me I smelled of beer.

I could tell you about the many nights I rubbed Kate's skin with oils to try to soothe it. The nights spent on the floor in her various hospital rooms, there just to listen to anything she might want to say. Running after nurses to get them to keep to the medication schedule or to let them know of spikes in her vital signs. The countless meals I made with burdock root and curcuma and cinnamon because maybe it might help. But every now and then I was irresponsible and self-destructive. Maybe because she was still with us and I wanted to remain a kid. Or maybe it was payback of some kind for all the wrongs she had done me or the times she was an irresponsible parent. When she forgot me at a party. When she told me I was mediocre. When she questioned my intelligence. Maybe it was a screwed-up way of showing her I still needed her.

Anyway, Kate flew home from London the morning after her birthday while I got my hungover self ready for the matinee performance of *Seven Deadly Sins*. She headed for the Royal Victoria Hospital for a new round of chemo or an ablation of the tumors on her liver while I danced around the Covent Garden stage, trying to hear the orchestra so I could find my note, making sure to avoid a flying foot that could take me out and keeping my muscles taut for when the male dancer needed to lift me over his head or I needed to kick my leg as high as I could without falling over onto my prima ballerina doppelgänger costar, Zenaida Yanowsky, who was two inches taller than me and a hundred inches thinner and stunningly beautiful.

Throughout her illness, people always said Kate was a "fighter." As if when you die you have somehow lost a battle that you could have won. Kate didn't have a chance. Her spirit and the medications prolonged her life, but when she eventually succumbed, it wasn't because she stopped fighting, but more because her time ran out and she allowed death to take her.

My mother was very rational, yet she was also spiritual, even a little religious. These two driving forces, her scientific mind and her faith (her faithy science), lent her a kind of grace in her long illness. After Kate was diagnosed, she quickly gave up the image of herself as an old lady and a grandmother and sought for ways to be as effective as she could with the time she had.

Now I live in her house and wear her clothes. I'm holding on as best I can, but every year I shed a little more of my mother. Her papers, her keepsakes, her pots and pans and other things are disappearing slowly, at the same time as my face grows to look more and more like hers. When she was sick, she asked the Grey Nuns to pray for her and they still send a letter every month to tell her, or rather me, that she is in their prayers. I haven't told them that she is gone. To make room for me and the kids, I have moved a lot of her things into a shed at the back of the apartment building. I've been meaning for years to clean the shed out and turn it into something, but for now it stores her.

Twelve

In the spring of 2009, I became pregnant. I was relieved, not only because I had always wanted children, but because I was so tired of myself and my career—worrying about whether I was doing enough and if I was good enough—I just wanted to put all my energy into someone else. There was maybe some magical thinking involved, too: I thought that if Kate could hang in until I got the baby into her arms, she would maybe live a little longer.

The due date was January 18, 2010, and we planned to have our baby in Montreal. A few of my friends had had their babies at home, but I didn't think Brad or Kate would be up for that, so I registered at a birthing center where I could give birth without any anesthesia, if possible—I was one of those— in a controlled environment where I would still be able to move around, or crouch, or kneel, or whatever was called for or reasonable in the situation. Because of my robust nature and physique, I naturally assumed the birth would go off without a hitch. Kate had had both Rufus and me in a matter of hours and without epidurals, either, though admittedly she always believed her labors were as fast as they were because she was hungover both times. I will leave that out there for the world to ponder, but not for too long.

Kate was always well enough to accompany Brad and me on our visits to the midwife, as well as to our twenty-week scan. I imagined myself caring for both my baby and my mother simultaneously. That was my hope, at least. Though she was clearly moving closer to the end point, I imagined we would have a year, maybe even two.

In the summer, I recorded an album of Édith Piaf songs called *Sans Fusils, Ni Souliers, à Paris*, which is a line from a Piaf song called "Les Grognards." I wanted to get something down because I knew that after the baby came, I wouldn't be able to write, record, and release a record of my own for a while. (This is the thing about a music career: even though I was relieved I had a beautiful excuse not to focus on it for a while, I was anxious to do enough that there was no risk people would forget me. Not to mention that I still needed money.) The Piaf record was a project of love. Hal Willner, the American producer who had pulled together both the Leonard Cohen tribute concert and *Leonard Cohen: I'm Your Man*, the record that flowed out of it, approached me to do the Piaf album, which was a great honor. We recorded it live over the course of three performances in June, in front a small audience at Dixon Place, a black box experimental theater space in the East Village.

The entire project was a wonderful experience, from singing the music of someone I had admired since I was a kid to working with Hal, which I had wanted to do for years. Growing up, we had listened to his album *Amarcord Nino Rota*—great jazz players interpreting the music of the composer who had worked with Fellini—on heavy rotation. On my Piaf album, the core band of Brad, Doug Wieselman, and Thomas Bartlett really shone, and, most importantly, Kate was there for all three performances, helping to pick the songs, singing and playing on a few numbers, and working with Hal and me to choose the final mixes.

On top of it all, I'd had an attachment to Piaf since I was a kid. She was a musical fixture in Quebec, but in classic Wainwright-McGarrigle form, Rufus and I probably were among the few of our generation who listened to her regularly. We would blare her music on the turntable, with "Milord" being a personal favorite. In the photos of Piaf in that little black dress, she always reminded me of my grandmother, Gaby. Whenever I'd asked Gaby about her youth, her answers were always set to a Piaf soundtrack in my childish mind. Piaf's spirit and her dark wildness appealed to me, too. My mother liked to tell us about how Piaf sang alone as a child on the street, and I always pictured myself in her thin shoes, in the snow, a slight figure bellowing out notes that cut through the air. I had sung along to her songs when I was a kid, but it wasn't until I tried to sing them myself that I realized how amazing she really was.

Piaf's name sometimes comes up when you type my name into a search engine, which makes me happy. When I went on tour for the album in 2010, after Kate had died, I always imagined both Piaf and my mom watching me perform from the balcony. Their collective gaze was loving but critical, and I wanted to make them proud. I didn't imagine them talking to each other, hanging out and drinking red wine and arguing or singing together—that would be silly. But it was easy to pretend that the silhouettes of two audience members in the balcony were Kate and Édith, which made me smile and also hold back tears.

Maybe Kate making the Piaf record with me was on her version of a "bucket list," along with Rufus taking her on the road as he did in those last few years. Of course, my mom had made great records and she had also traveled extensively herself over the course of her own career, but she certainly sought out and appreciated these experiences with her kids. Rufus also took her to Venice for the Biennale where they floated along the canals at four in the morning on their way to another party. And she made it to the premiere of his first opera, *Prima Donna*, at the Manchester festival in 2009, which was important to him. In a way, everything Rufus had done was dedicated to her. In some respects, Kate was his muse.

Sometimes she went too far in her travels and exhausted herself, but for her, it was better than staying in bed. In this same way, she threw herself into planning and preparing for the 2009 McGarrigles Christmas show. Inspired by *The McGarrigle Christmas Hour* album released in 2005, these annual shows had become an epic Christmas family madness, all the brainchild of Kate. We'd appeared on some great stages, even Carnegie Hall—but this time Kate was pouring all her artistic and physical energy into bringing it home for a Dickensian extravaganza at the Royal Albert Hall in London, with guests such as Boy George, Guy Garvey from Elbow, Linda Thompson, Brian Eno, and Ed Harcourt, the comedy duo French and Saunders, and the family—herself, Anna, and Rufus, as well as Sloan Wainwright and Lily. These family shows are an exhibition of the family business of singing and playing, but they are also a true expression of our ties. They involve months of planning and many (maybe not always enough) rehearsals and are where we are able to spend time together, in harmony and sometimes in conflict. Anyone who's seen one of these shows knows that they are not highly produced, rehearsed, and orchestrated events. They are often a little rocky and emotional, often funny, and always revealing, with beautiful musical moments and a lot of courageous song choices.

Kate was writing a new song for the occasion, which became the soundtrack of her experience from that moment forward and later an anthem for our family. It's a song that has an impact on many who hear it, but for me it held a special meaning because I like to think I played a role in her writing it, in that the mother and the daughter struggle to return to each other. The song is about the seasons, and why we have them, based on the myth of Proserpina (Persephone) and her mother's desperate longing for her. After Hades abducts Proserpina and brings her to the underworld, her mother is in such despair that Zeus strikes a deal with Hades, which allows Proserpina to be with her mother for half the year. (Like a custody battle, or maybe that's just how I see it right now.) Each time she returns, she brings life back to the world through spring. When she has to go back to her husband, her mother renders the world barren, which is why we all suffer through winter. Especially in Canada.

Since the song is about seasons, my mother turned the story into a Christmas carol. But it is also a repetitive prayer that refers to several painful truths in Kate's life at the time: her own death; her return to her own mother, Gaby; her return to Mother Earth; her own daughter's straying and absence and return; and ultimately her belief and hope in the cycle of life that she will now join in her death. That song felt like she was calling to me, and in the weeks leading up to its premiere onstage, her calling could not have been any louder, foretelling a future that was directly in front of us.

As Kate performed her song—only once, it turned out, on that stage in London—she was already on her way to her own underworld or otherworld. Most likely she believed it was nowhere. But with her song, she helped us accept and believe that she was on her way to another place. One that she was meant to go to. In this way, she made her final months and eventual death a religious experience.

Then there is what she did for strangers, setting up the Kate McGarrigle Fund to raise money for cancer research with a focus on sarcoma, the kind of cancer she had. It was too late for her, she knew, but she wanted to help those who would be suffering in the future. Clear cell sarcoma often affects young people and she was upset about that. Having a degree in science, and having friends who were scientists, she was interested in playing a part and raising money for research.

Getting out there, having fun with her kids, hobnobbing, working, writing, and thinking about other people. In truth, Kate was generally a little selfish, but she wanted to give something to the world before she left it, and she didn't want to be forgotten. Time was running out and she was running alongside it as fast as she could.

We had all accepted the fact that I wouldn't be able to be part of the Christmas show in London on December 9. It was just too close to my due date. Instead, I would nest in our apartment in Montreal and buy little clothes, fold them obsessively, take baths, and apply cream to my expanding belly while waiting for the big push. We did not know the sex of the baby. I wanted to be surprised at the birth.

Still, I had agreed to make a last trip to London, Paris, and Belgium in early November to perform some shows promoting the Piaf album. Before we left, Brad and I visited the midwife. She was slightly unhappy that the baby was transverse lie, meaning that it was in a sideways position across my belly, but she also told us that the baby had plenty of time to get into the head-down position necessary for a vaginal birth. Otherwise, everything seemed fine, so we flew to London.

We were staying in my music managers' nice company flat in Camden Town. I spent the first few days after we landed hiring small string and horn sections for the first of two London shows, which was to be at the Barbican. I also went to Topshop to find something to wear, the goal being not to hide my bump but to show it off. I did a great photo shoot and some press, and then the show, all of which were a success. I remember a brief moment of feeling like I had it all.

I was getting bigger every day, and I loved that. I was also getting more Braxton-Hicks contractions, which I had been told was completely normal during this stage of pregnancy. I had been having those contractions for some time, in fact. Oddly, I didn't feel the baby moving around much, just those Braxton-Hicks tightenings of the uterine muscles.

The morning after the concert, I had a couple of BBC interviews to do. My stomach felt much harder than it had before, and the baby was still in the transverse position—I could feel the head pushing hard on one side, which was uncomfortable. Thomas Bartlett, my great friend and extremely talented musical collaborator, had come along with me, and at one point I placed his hand on the side of my belly so he could feel how hard it was. He seemed grossed out.

Brad was only staying for the second London show, at the Pigalle Club in Piccadilly, then he was flying home with Thomas, leaving me to go on to Paris and Belgium for three days with a tour manager. By the time of my own flight home, I would be thirty-one weeks, with nine weeks to go.

Before the show at the Pigalle, we had some Indian food, and afterward my stomach felt a little strange. Chalking it up to the meal, I walked over to the club to get ready. In my dressing room, I painted my nails red, just one coat. I never paint my nails, but I didn't play the guitar in the Piaf show and the material called for a little more of a gussied-up look.

This show was for the press and a small audience of around

two hundred serious fans who'd snatched up the tickets. Onstage, it was just the three of us—Brad, Thomas, and me. I started feeling more and more pain in my lower abdomen, but I pushed through the songs as best as I could. The contractions were sharper than the ones I'd been having, and also lower down. At one point, I reached for a stool onstage to steady myself, and the audience gasped. I assured them it was just false labor, and that I was feeling great. But I wasn't.

Back in the apartment after the show, I put on my pajamas. The cramps were still coming, more painfully than before. I noticed I was starting to bleed a little bit after each one. Worried, I called the midwife in Montreal, who told me to get to the nearest hospital right away. I looked up the names of London hospitals, and I picked University College London Hospital, which was close by and sounded good to me because it was tied to the university, something I had learned to appreciate from the last few years of Kate being in and out of the hospital.

Brad and I set off in a black cab. In the emergency room, the staff saw me very quickly, which surprised and further alarmed me. A lot of people in that emergency room looked much worse off than I did, but when you're pregnant, I guess they fast-track you. After they took my vitals, they brought me upstairs in a wheelchair. I thought they were going to recommend I cancel the rest of my trip, fly home, and put my feet up for a couple of weeks of bed rest. Instead they set me up in a private room with a monitor on my belly to track the baby's heart rate. It was two in the morning by now, and the cramps were coming every ten minutes or so. First a nurse, then a resident, and then an ultrasound technician came in to look at me. Each one in turn would call for someone else. Eventually, one of the technicians took an interior ultrasound, in which they put what they call a wand up your vagina so they can see the baby better. More and more people were coming into my room to stare at the screen, and I was getting more and more upset. A few minutes after the wand examination, my water broke.

I was scared, an emotion everyone else in the room seemed to share because almost immediately they switched into a different mode: *anxious*. A consensus seemed to be reached that we needed to wait until the big-gun obstetrician showed up at 6 a.m., since both the resident and the technician had spotted something on the baby's back that concerned them, some kind of blurring on the spine, and the baby was still transverse lie, tucked over on one side. That's when Brad and I first heard the words "spina bifida." But, I protested, at the twenty-week scan, there'd been no indication of anything abnormal, and wouldn't it have detected something like that? At this point, Dr. Janet Rennie showed up—our big-gun neonatal specialist. She would become our guide through an ordeal that would last for months.

That morning, Dr. Rennie spoke to us about spina bifida and how it can affect a baby. The scale ranged from very low to very extreme. In its worst cases, it carried the potential for paralysis and severe brain damage. Brad and I both burst into tears. We were exhausted and petrified and in the process of scheduling another more in-depth scan when I called my mother, something I'd been hoping I wouldn't have to do.

It was the middle of the night in Montreal. Kate was asleep

on the couch, her favorite place, when the phone rang. When I explained the situation to her, she told me she would get on a plane. At the time, she was very sick, much more sick than I knew. I hadn't seen her for two weeks, during which her illness had escalated. The cancer was spreading, the days were getting shorter, the leaves were falling from the trees, and it was becoming clear that her death was coming sooner than anyone expected or wanted. (*Proserpina, Proserpina, come home to mama, come home to mama now.*)

I have to admit, I had skipped all the chapters related to preterm birth in the books I had read during my pregnancy. I never once doubted I would carry my baby to full term, confident that my body would never fail me. I had done everything right. I hadn't drunk a drop of alcohol, I had exercised and eaten really well. Nothing bad had ever happened to me, health-wise. I was always physically strong, and I'd tested normal for pretty much everything my whole life. Average across the board, really. Average in height and weight. Average at school. Average number of boyfriends. Average in looks and average in sports. Average in everything. I was definitely not used to being different or outstanding, and certainly not infirm. In fact, I had always fought for attention, and now I was getting way too much and the wrong kind.

At last, I asked Dr. Rennie what my baby's chances were, dreading the answer. I had no idea what a thirty-week-old baby looked like or what their level of development was. She told us that at thirty weeks the organs are just about formed, and that it is a viable age for not only survival but going on to live a regular life, that is, provided the spina bifida wasn't there.

Dr. Rennie soon sent me for another, more close-up scan. This sonographer wasn't totally convinced she was seeing spina bifida, which granted us the right to hope that it might not be that after all. The contractions had stopped, but the placenta was near the opening of the cervix, and there was a risk it would start to drop out and pull dangerously on the umbilical cord. Also, there was no amniotic fluid left; our baby had to get born. I was booked for an emergency cesarean section in the hospital operating room that afternoon. There was no reason to wait.

The nurse gave me a shot of vitamin K for the baby's lungs, which are the last organs to develop, and then they prepped me for surgery. I called my mother again to tell her the plan, and she said she had a reservation for the next morning.

Knowing that she was on her way, I allowed myself to feel what was true and in my heart. I was going to have a baby, something I had wanted and dreamed about since my early twenties. I'd always wanted children. I'm just wired that way, and still am. I told Brad then that whatever happened, and whatever the state our baby was in, I was happy; the two of us would be great parents who would do everything we could to help our child. My state of mind and my focus had shifted completely, from fear to the extreme love a mother feels when she thinks about her baby.

* * *

I was feeling weirdly chatty when I came into the operating room. As the anesthesiologist was tapping my spine for the epidural, I told him that now I *would* be able to participate in the Christmas show at the Royal Albert Hall, since it didn't look like I would be leaving London anytime soon. It was going to be our biggest show yet, I said, and he should come! He humored me with a faint smile and a slight nod of agreement. As he started the drip, my teeth began to chatter as they often do when I take drugs, and he assured me that this was normal. Then Brad came in, looking dashing in his light-blue scrubs. Over the last twelve hours, Brad and I had clung to each other like scared children. That night we were closer than we had ever been.

The surgery took longer than usual because the baby was pinched behind one of my hip bones or something. I never really understood what was going on from a technical standpoint. All I knew was that I required a classical C-section, the most invasive of the three possible options, which involved a vertical incision. It was explained to me that now that I'd undergone a classical cesarean, I could never have a vaginal birth because of the heightened risk of my uterus rupturing, and I told them that if they had to chop my head off to get the baby out safely, that would be fine with me. When I looked up cesareans online later on, I discovered that one of the reasons they were developed was to deliver a baby from a dead mother because it wasn't socially acceptable to bury a woman with a baby in utero. In my more rational moments, I believe that in a life-or-death childbirth situation, a doctor should save a mother's life first, but at the time, I didn't seem to care much about my body, or about any pain I might be feeling, or even about the potential of my own death.

When my baby was lifted out of me and cried, and they told me he was a boy, I was in heaven. Here he was, and he was real.

They took him straight to the examining table, where a team of six doctors and as many nurses gave him a detailed looking over. They seemed calm, and I could hear the baby making noises, which I assumed was good. After a while, one of them told me they wanted to give him oxygen to regulate his breathing. They also confirmed there was something on his back—a big bruise, it looked like, but they weren't sure. Then they wrapped him up and showed him to me for the first time.

I'm not sure if I was thinking normally, or if whatever went through my mind was compounded by the situation or that he looked so small or that preemies can look like very old people, but his face felt like one I'd known all my life. I was overwhelmed and extremely happy to be his mother. Then I got a dose of morphine directly into my spine, and that made me even happier...

From that point on, the plan, and my responsibility, was perfectly clear. I was this baby's mother. I was surprised and pleased when one of the doctors asked me if I was planning on nursing, because I'd assumed that the baby had arrived too soon for that to happen. But they told me it was not only possible, but it would be a good thing to do, too.

I took this, my first job as a mother, very seriously. They told me it would take longer than normal for my milk to come in, since my body hadn't yet been getting ready for it. After a few tutorials, I set to work kneading my boobs with my fists. It was painful, but I didn't care, and neither was I aware of any pain from my incision since I was so focused on my baby.

Arcangelo was the name Brad and I had been kicking around for the past couple of months. It was Brad's maternal grandfather's name, and when I'd heard it for the first time, I'd told Brad it would be a great name for a baby. Brad's mom was surprised that I wanted to name our boy after her father, figuring the name was too Italian. But I liked that. Brad had been named after Marion's mother, Bradamante, and I'd always tried to get him to go by his full name. (He never went for it, having absorbed his relatives' sense that Italians in America should Americanize as best they could.) We called our baby Arc for short, which undercut the glory of Arcangelo a little, but gave him another angle—blond surfer dude.

A few hours after I came out of surgery, one of the doctors came to tell us that she didn't think the baby had spina bifida—that it was some kind of giant bruise, or hemangioma. Before doing anything more, they had to make sure it wasn't something else with blood vessels that would draw from his heart. Still, over the next few days, they seemed to accept that it was an anomaly—a large bruise, maybe, caused by Arc getting stuck and triggering my early labor. The other thing that pointed to a position problem was that when Arc arrived, he was completely curved over. He had what's known as a kyphosis, essentially a hunchback. For the first few weeks of his life, he wasn't allowed to lie on his back, only on his side. There were also a couple of holes in his heart that would either repair themselves or we would have to have repaired later, and some other small things the doctors and nurses were monitoring constantly. Still, overall, everyone was confident he would survive, and Brad and I began to breathe more easily.

In stark contrast to this hopeful outcome, there was Kate.

Thirteen

KATE MATERIALIZED IN LONDON a day after Arcangelo was born. She was truly, visibly dying by then. It was almost as though she came to London in order to pass the baton to Arc before stopping the race herself, like a handoff, a transference of life.

She came straight to the hospital from the airport. Arc was out of the NICU by then, and we'd been moved to the neonatal unit, where we were surrounded by half a dozen other babies. Some stayed for just a day, and some were there for months; some left the hospital, some didn't. That evening, when Kate arrived, we were feeling stunned and scared and sad and hopeful. My mom, I remember, wore a mask, not to protect Arc and the other babies, but to protect herself. Her cancer had spread to the bone and she'd begun radiation.

She had rushed to be with me and to see her grandson, but I also had a sense that this trip was a kind of completion or resolution of a tragedy that had haunted my mother her whole life. Kate hadn't had just two babies, Rufus and me. She'd had three. Her firstborn son had died at a hospital in Euston, less than a mile from where the two of us were now, when Kate was twenty-four. Over the years, she had spoken about the experience in her most vulnerable moments. When I was old enough to really understand the story she was telling me, it became clear it was the most traumatic event of her life.

As I wrote earlier, my dad left for England when my mom was six months pregnant, and she followed him, not sure whether he planned to return to her or not. When my dad came to meet Arc a month or so later, he walked me along Euston Road, off Regent's Park, and pointed out the building where their first son was born, three months premature. He described my mother screaming in pain as she labored for the longest time, and how the little boy they named James only survived for a few hours. He remembered signing the birth certificate at the same time he had to sign the death certificate, and also told me that the baby was buried not far from the hospital. It was in the midst of her grief that Kate developed the peritonitis that almost killed her; she blamed the bath she was given right after the birth. When she'd recovered, the doctors told her the infection had scarred her interior so badly that she would not be able to have more children. She'd left London for Saint-Sauveur then, and my dad didn't go with her. I don't know why he didn't, and it makes me angry still. The experience almost destroyed her, and it was another six months before she physically recovered. That terrible time, along with her love for Loudon and his rejection of her, inspired a few of Kate's most well-known and powerful songs, including "Tell My Sister," which is the one of hers I sing in concert the most

(*Tell my sister to tell my mother I'm coming home...alone*), and
"Go Leave," where she sings about another woman.

> *Go, leave*
> *She's better than me*
> *Or at least she is stronger*
> *She will make it last longer*
> *That's nice for you....*
> *I remember days when we laughed a lot*
> *Those that weren't so good I soon forgot*
> *We could sit and talk till words*
> *Were coming out our ears*
> *Not just for days or weeks or months*
> *But it's been years*
> *Now here they come*
> *Here come my tears*

In the recording on *Kate & Anna McGarrigle*, Kate accompanies herself masterfully on the guitar. It is only her and the instrument and as she plays the very last note you can hear a tiny bell ring out. Kate told me it was the sound of a tear falling on the string. It cut me up pretty hard.

I don't know how and when these songs came out of her mind and body, but that's what they sound like—like they are coming out of all of her. Kate and Anna would release that debut five years later, but that is what is often so amazing about first records. They hold a lot of experience in them because they are the first major expression of an artist and so much change happens in a person's late teens and twenties, releasing enough energy to be explosive.

I guess she and my dad did love each other, though, because eventually they got back together. They'd been through life and death at a young age, and they had to have been shaken. Dad's telling of this story is a little different, but I remember how my mother recounted her story through tears of sorrow on several occasions, so I choose to tell her account. Besides, who else will? The good news is that even though the doctors had told Kate she couldn't get pregnant, three years later she gave birth to Rufus, and three years after that, to me.

At the hospital with me and my new baby, Kate told me she felt lighter about James dying because Arc was going to survive. This consoled her. Before she died, she had held her grandson in her arms just a half mile from where she had lost her first child forty years before.

I don't know how I managed it, but I was still in denial that my mom was so close to the end. Arc and most of the other babies had developed postnatal jaundice and were being kept under jaundice lamps. Perhaps because I was out of my mind at the time, I wondered if those lamps could help my mom's jaundice, too. Kate was very yellow and frail, and her stomach was distended with fluid. Could I somehow get Kate into an incubator? Could I help her grow instead of fade away? When I asked the doctors, they looked at me as if I were crazy. No, they said, the lamps would not work on her.

Still, I think my mom was revived by the fact that we needed her. She didn't want to touch the baby too much since he was so small, but she loved to gaze at him. Mostly she sat with me. We spent time surveying our battered bodies. She had Xs in permanent marker on her shoulder and back from her recent radiation. The scar from my C-section, which was stapled and on the large side, didn't compare to the giant chevron scar that covered the entire front of her torso, but the two of us still felt a kind of kinship. Or maybe it was just the joy of being a mom with your mom.

Kate was able to stay for four or five days before she had to fly home for another radiation treatment, and also to prepare for the Christmas concert, for which she'd be on another flight to London in a couple of weeks. Even though she was exhausted and in pain, she managed to be there for me and for Brad, who'd gotten very down. He was having a hard time dealing with the stress of a baby who had to remain in the hospital. He'd never liked London and felt angry that we were stuck there, and that he now had the job of finding us a flat close to the hospital. My mother kept trying to lift his spirits, saying things like "London is a great town. It's beautiful and there are great museums and you have friends here." But he didn't want to hear it, and I got angry that this woman who was dying was trying to cheer my husband up. She even tried to help Brad find a suitable flat, visiting a couple with him. She saw the cracks in our relationship clearly, and she did everything she could to help, right up to the moment Mercedes had to drive her to the airport and put her on a plane.

Years later, Mercedes told me that when she dropped my

mom off at the airport after that trip, Kate said that I would eventually come to my senses when it came to my marriage, but that now wasn't the time to leave Brad. She had been so kind to him, but she had seen that I was in a lot of pain. I wish she had told me that herself, and sometimes wonder if she had wanted to, but time ran out before she could.

Brad eventually found us a place off Baker Street, about a mile from the hospital, and the two weeks before Kate would be back for the Christmas concert went by pretty quickly. I would walk from the flat to the hospital and back again four times a day to feed Arc, which was good exercise and also helped me mentally. My milk had finally come in, and my job now was to be a cow. I would pump away at the hospital and also at home, half a dozen times a day. I set my alarm for the middle of the night so I could bring the milk I'd pumped over to the hospital, often passing by 221B Baker Street, the home of Sherlock Holmes, in the dead of night.

I went back to the hospital every morning. They let me take Arc out of the incubator for forty-five minutes at a time to feed him by tube and to have "kangaroo time," holding him against my chest under my shirt. The closeness, the warmth, the smell, and the sound of a parent's heartbeat is known to help preemies thrive, but I have to say it does a lot for the parent, too. Brad did it, also, and it really helped him feel involved. I spent as much time as possible taking care of Arc in whatever way I could, changing his diaper through the armholes in the incubator (the one coat of nail polish from my night of singing Piaf chipping away), feeding him by tube, and eventually practicing nursing, which took a month for him to learn how to do. Arc had to get strong enough to be able to manage. At first, he would suck for just a few seconds and then need to take a nap.

I walked back and forth, back and forth, from flat to hospital, from hospital to flat, as Christmas decorations were lit on the streets and Central London breathed in and out. I breathed with it. It felt good to have something—anything—to occupy myself with. Brad had nothing to do but worry and be sad and scared. To be honest, I couldn't help him much either. All my energy was going to Arc, and to fending off the guilt I felt over abandoning my mother in her last days.

One day, Brad got drunk on Baileys and ended up writhing on the floor, holding his chest and exclaiming that he was having a heart attack. I asked him over and over if he wanted me to call an ambulance, though I was sure he wasn't having a heart attack, just in need for attention. I had to get back to Arc at the hospital and had very little patience for him. What was *he* so upset about? *My* mother was dying; *I* was going back and forth to the hospital to nurse. *I* was healing from surgery. *I* was paying for everything. Why was he having a heart attack? It was almost like he felt powerless and it totally flipped him out.

On December 4, Kate and the whole clan arrived in London for final rehearsals. She, Rufus, and Lily rented a small, drafty cottage in Sloane Square, where my mom spent most of the time resting under blankets on the sitting room couch.

There, Lorca came to visit because she and Rufus had decided they wanted to be parents together and were trying to conceive a baby. Crazy times! Rufus really wanted Kate's approval and enthusiasm for this plan, but Kate didn't seem too interested in things that belonged to a future she wouldn't be around to experience. She had time only to live in the present in a world that was getting smaller and smaller. I know she wanted Rufus and me to be happy, but she never spoke about what our future might look like without her. In fact, she didn't want to talk at all about her death and what it meant to her or to anybody else. All we had were gestures and silent tears shed. The holding of hands and the reminiscing had begun. Though the hospital had strict rules about visitors for Arc—beyond Brad and me, it was only supposed to be grandparents—my family and friends showed up like a gypsy caravan and lied about who was who.

It soon became clear that Kate couldn't really rehearse, after putting in one session with the choir, which was made up of a lot of my girlfriends, like Mercedes, Varie, and Emma, along with various old friends of Kate's and Anna's. She called Brian Eno in to help with harmonies, but he quickly confessed that he was rubbish at teaching actual parts, so Kate stepped right up to do it, summoning people to her couch. She wanted the four-part harmony in "Old Waits Carol" to be just right.

"Proserpina," though, was easy. The singers created a rousing Greek chorus just the way Kate imagined it. But she also wanted to do another song, "In the Bleak Midwinter," and that one proved to be more difficult. As its title suggests, the song is about the birth of Christ during the most barren time of the year. Even though it's about birth, in true McGarrigle/Wainwright fashion, our arrangement sounded very deathy. But it does also mention archangels, which added to its poignancy for us. Maybe that is why Kate wanted to add it. In the past year, she had been returning to all things mystical and religious. Was Arcangelo our baby Jesus? Or perhaps she was thinking that the immaculate turkey-baster conception of Rufus and Lorca's baby would be our miracle? She never said. But the plan was for Rufus and me to sing "In the Bleak Midwinter" with her, and in an effort maybe designed to stop time, or at least slow it down, she played it over and over at rehearsal, making us sing it a hundred times. It was hard to get the three-part harmony. I had trouble finding the notes, which made it harder for her. She would sometimes become confused, and a few times she needed to lie down. We sang and sang:

> *Angels and archangels*
> *May have gathered there*
> *Cherubim and seraphim thronged the air*
> *But only his mother in her maiden bliss*
> *Worshipped the beloved*
> *With a kiss*

But it was the lyric *Come home to mama* from "Proserpina" that had the strongest call, everything at this time taking on a heightened sense of meaning. People would come into the sitting room with Kate to rehearse—Boy George, Guy Garvey, French and Saunders, Ed Harcourt, and the many friends in the choir—as we ran over "Proserpina" like a mantra. Swaying and looking to our leader for guidance, we were Kate's congregation.

And then, finally, it was the night of the show.

It's hard to explain what took place that evening, but it was magical, and everyone who was there onstage or in the audience felt it, too. I did a very good rendition of the gospel song "Mary Had a Baby" and made a speech thanking the NHS for taking care of me and Arc, which got a round of cheers. Brad was playing bass, and helping lead the band. Rufus was stellar as usual. And Sloan brought the house down. But the real show was Kate. We held her arms as she mounted the stage, which she graced with regal poise for the next two hours. For her last performance, my mom conjured up everything she had. We'd done her makeup and her hair, and had wrapped her in her favorite silk shantung dress, and she looked like a queen on her throne, or the god or goddess Anna told us she always wanted to be. The highlight, of course, was "Proserpina." It had been a long time since she'd sung with that much power. Kate had always loved Christmas, and here she was on England's most famous stage, riding her chariot of fire with all three of her children, the two living and the one no longer alive, her new grandson, and the people who mattered the most to her.

The next morning, Kate stopped to say goodbye on the way to the airport. Brad brought us tea while the two of us lay together on the bed. I remember we quarreled about replacing the outside stairs on Querbes; the metal was corroded, the wood was rotten and untrustworthy, and they were a menace to anyone who climbed them. I insisted that Kate get the stairs fixed so she wouldn't fall and end up in a wheelchair, a danger with her ever-deteriorating bones. Kate just looked at me sadly and began to cry. "It doesn't matter," she said. At that moment, we both understood that she would be climbing those stairs only once more. When she went down them again, someone would be carrying her body.

Only one photo exists of my mom holding Arc. Somehow, in the midst of everything, Brad had had the presence of mind to take Arc out of his incubator and place him carefully in her arms. Then he used the digital camera Kate carried around with her in her last year of life to take their portrait. After she died, that camera became something of an art piece. Some of the photos she took are ordinary, in the sense they show loved ones and big events, but many documented her last travels. A room in Venice, a part of Hadrian's Wall. All of those are both beautiful and sad. She'd had to erase a couple of her images to make room for the photo of her and Arc, which was hard for her. At that point, everything was a farewell. Everything was being erased.

Fourteen

AFTER MY MOTHER HAD GONE home, my whole focus was on helping Arc grow bigger and stronger. The sooner that happened, the sooner we could return to Montreal. We spent Christmas morning with Arc at the hospital. The staff passed out mini Santa hats for the babies—thanks to the hospital volunteers, there was always a steady stream of ridiculously small knitted hats and sweaters for the preemies—and Brad and I added a new small stuffed animal to Arc's bed, along with the little Saint Bernard Kate had bought him at the hospital's gift shop. As he grew strong enough to nurse, his clothes became less doll-sized. I knew that even as my baby grew, my mother was weakening, moving ever closer to the end.

I missed Kate terribly, and began negotiating with the doctors about when it would be safe enough for Arc to make the trip. So far, they wouldn't allow it. I tried everything to persuade them; we'd even done a simulation in a little portable unit like Doctor Who's phone box that mimicked the air pressure on an airplane, but Arc's breathing became distressed. He wasn't ready yet. So just after Christmas, I left him for a couple of days to see Kate.

The family had gathered at St. Sauveur for the holiday. Kate had been able to come downstairs on Christmas night and sit at the table for an hour or so. But when I got there, Kate was back in her bed, which had been her mother's bed before her, the room making room for more ghosts.

She had always loved baths, and when I asked if she wanted me to give her one, she said yes. I ran the water in the same tub she was washed in as a kid. In the bright bathroom, we took off her clothes. Her body was still very handsome and young-looking, but her skin had a permanent yellow hue, and of course there was the giant scar. She seemed glad to be in the water. She had only a few simple joys left. Food had become a burden, and sleep was more tiresome than it was rejuvenating. I sat with her as she soaked, pumping away with my little hand pump to make sure I kept my milk supply up for Arc, and we talked about when I could finally come home, whom she had seen at Christmas, what I was like as a baby, what schools I went to. Mostly, though, I let her talk about her past and other things. She let long silences fall between words, because by now no unnecessary words were spoken.

Later, Kate asked Lily to take a picture of us. Photos were proof that she was still here, as well as a way of stopping time. For her sixtieth birthday, only three years earlier, she had written an incredible song called "I Just Want to Make It Last." She already knew she was dying and the recording that she made of herself on the piano in her living room is gut-wrenching.

Make that earth slow down a bit
As it spins around the sun
It's going awful fast
And I'm having too much fun...
So make the earth slow down a bit
We're going way too fast—
And I just want it to last.

The day finally came when Brad and I were allowed to walk out of that hospital with our baby. First, though, Arc and I were sent to the maternity unit where new mothers spend a couple of nights with their newborns after labor. It was a space where only curtains separated the women in their beds. Most of the others were in pain or exhausted and fumbling around with all these tiny new beings who were both frightening and irresistible. The babies cried incessantly and so did some of the new moms.

Having almost lived at the hospital for the past month and a half, I breezed around as if I owned the joint. While Arc napped peacefully in his cot, I visited the other moms, gently volunteering my help. I didn't want to annoy them, but I had so much I could show them. One of my neighbors had had twins, and I coached her on how to drag her nipple over one of her baby's lips to see if he would latch on. I offered to sit with babies so their mothers could go pee or just shut their eyes for a few minutes. Basically, I *was* annoying, and so happy and proud of myself as I strode along the corridors, Arc in one arm, trying to boost the spirits of the other moms. I sneaked my dad in past visiting hours to meet his grandson. He was very happy but maybe a little weary—songs are where the drama of life and family must live, not here in the light of night.

On the second morning, Brad arrived and helped me pack all our things, and then we sat there on the bed waiting for the nurse to discharge us, feeling a little unreal. Right before we were about to leave—Arc was strapped into his baby carrier—one of the nurses stopped in, offering to show us how to do infant CPR. She explained that staff weren't always able to teach this to new parents, but it was a rare quiet time on her ward. I was eager to get out of there, but decided another ten minutes wouldn't hurt.

She demonstrated on a doll she fetched from a closet. She explained that if Arc ever turned blue and went floppy, we should first try to clear his airway by turning him over and patting him on the back. If that didn't work, she showed us how to do very, very careful mouth-to-mouth. If you breathed too hard, a tiny baby's lungs could explode. Count to five, and then do it again. If that failed, she demonstrated how to compress his tiny chest by placing a hand a distance of four fingers down from his throat and gently but firmly pressing down, releasing, and pressing again. Just when I thought we were free to go, she insisted that both Brad and I try all of this out on the doll. When it was over, Brad and I practically flew out of there, rushing home for our first day as a new family in the little flat on Baker Street.

That afternoon, Brad was making dinner. As whatever he

was cooking bubbled away on the stove, we gave Arc a bath and then rubbed him down with oil and powder. I wrapped him up and brought him over to the couch to nurse. Soon, Brad and I began to argue about something, and he came over to sit beside me. I was leaning in to make a point when I noticed that Arc had stopped sucking. In fact, he wasn't moving at all and he was blue around the mouth. I moved him a little. He was floppy. Brad and I stared at each other in panic.

I said, "Okay?" and he said "Okay" back. I laid Arc over my knee and gently swatted him on his back. Once, twice, three times. Nothing. He was getting bluer.

I got off the couch, laid Arc on the floor, and again looked to Brad. "Okay?" I said. And Brad said, "Okay." Then he got on his phone and called 999.

I did exactly what the nurse had taught me only a few hours earlier. I put my mouth over Arc's whole nose and face, the technique for small babies, and carefully blew. Once, twice, three times. Nothing happened. Arc's eyes were closed, and he was even bluer. I heard sirens in the distance. Whenever there's a call about a baby, a police escort runs in front of the ambulance, clearing and shooing away cars and people. But help wasn't here yet.

The nurse had said the next step was chest compressions, but instead I tried the mouth-to-mouth one last time, and Arc started to move a little. He didn't exactly gasp, but his eyes started rolling around. Brad was still on the phone to 999; I grabbed it from him and described what I was seeing, and the nice woman on the other end kept asking if my baby was breathing, and my answer was yes, except he wasn't breathing normally or well. I kept repeating "His brain! His brain!" because I was desperately worried that it was being deprived of oxygen.

The paramedics who crashed into our tiny flat seemed surprised by how small Arc was. A normal-sized mask was way too big, so one of them positioned the mask so it kind of hovered over his whole face. Then they grabbed him, and Brad and I grabbed our coats, and we all piled into the back of the ambulance. The paramedics laid Arc on top of the gurney, which seemed gigantic, and told me to steady him there with my hand so he wouldn't fall off. I could see that his color still wasn't right, and that his eyes kept rolling back into his head, and I put my face close to his and pleaded with him to stay with us, please stay with us. I begged him over and over again. I glanced at Brad, who looked so stunned it was like he wasn't even there. I was sure we were going to lose our baby, like my mother had lost hers, and the paramedics made no attempt to convince me otherwise.

But at the hospital, they were able to stabilize him. The doctor on call that night asked me how long Arc had been unconscious, and when I told him that it was somewhere between one to two minutes, he assured me that babies as young as Arc have a lot of oxygen in their blood and can be without air even longer without suffering any lasting harm. He told me I had done exactly the right thing. He also told me I'd saved Arc, but I'm sure he was just trying to make me feel better.

My dad was still in London. I called him and he came right

away. I was sitting in a chair next to Arc in the emergency area, surrounded by sick and dying people, when I saw him arrive, but I couldn't get up. My dad took my hand, and I just pushed my face into his hip and started crying. "I can't do this," I said. "They should just take the baby away from me, because I don't know if I can manage." My dad didn't say anything. He just looked down at me, squeezing my hand, knowing how scared I was.

Until that point, I had not let what had been happening break me, but now I was broken. I asked that we be readmitted to the hospital, and they found a spare room for Arc and me in the children's cancer ward, which is one of the saddest places on earth. They hooked Arc back up to monitors and drips, and for the next few days, I was mute and almost frozen. It was determined that Arc had severe acid reflux, which could have caused him to regurgitate and choke. Fucking acid reflux put us back in the hospital? I didn't trust myself to do anything. I slept on the floor next to my son, and I told him that he and I couldn't go home for a while because I was just too scared. My eyes, I remember, were constantly wet. Not from weeping, exactly, but from some slow and steady flow of sorrow.

I didn't want to tell Kate what had happened and why we were back in the hospital. But after a couple of days, I needed her to know. Kate was quiet in response, almost disinterested, and when I told her I couldn't come home yet but was planning on flying in two weeks, she said, "All right, dear, I'll see you tomorrow."

All right, I'll see you tomorrow?

It had begun. The toxic cancer chemicals were moving to her brain. I'd been warned that when the patient stops making sense, they are near the end. I said, "Okay, Mom," and hung up. As the lights of the London night shone in the dark room among eerily empty and small hospital beds, I realized that she might not yet be dead, but she was gone and I was alone. I wept loudly for a little while, then I took a deep breath and returned to my son. With bleary eyes, I watched the screens that showed Arc's heart rate and blood oxygen levels, and I listened for alarms from the devices stuck to his tiny chest, then looked out the window toward Euston Station and, beyond that, Primrose Hill. What a terribly sad place I was in on this ward. But on the other hand, also an incredibly good place, and I struggled to feel hope.

Then there was the issue of money. After Arc was born, I had called my agent to see if he could get me a gig of any sort after I'd had a chance to recover a bit from the cesarean. I knew that the flat on Baker Street and London life in general was going to be expensive, and I needed to find a way to pay for it all. He booked me two nights at the Jazz Cafe. The dates arrived while we were back in the hospital, and now I had to do what I'd promised.

I left Arc in the good hands of the nurses, dropped by the flat to grab an outfit and my guitar, and hailed a cab. I wore a Japanese short kimono and striped pants, maybe inspired by the clowns who came to visit the kids on the cancer ward. And that night I was very zany. I cracked a lot of jokes and sang well. A good review I later read remarked on my theatrical stage presence, though the writer also questioned whether my songwriting would ever rise to the level of my father's or brother's.

After the show, I smoked a cigarette and drank a couple pints and laughed and hung out backstage with Sam, my tour manager, until closing, like I was myself again. I just wasn't ready to return to the hospital. But when I did, walking into Arc's room with all the monitors going, I felt that I could cope again, as if the show had rejuvenated and reinforced me, and reminded me of what I had to do: go out and play and support my child and come back better and stronger. *That* is who I was meant to be.

A week later, Arc and I went home. Disconnected from the medical apparatus, from now on our baby would need to lean on the apparatus of his parents. On that warm January day, Brad and I also took Arc to Regent's Park on his first outing so he could feel the sun on his yellow-tinged skin. And that was where Rufus reached me to say that Kate was dying.

After Arc and I had gone back into the hospital, my mom stopped eating. Rufus and my aunt Teddy had moved into Querbes to take care of her, along with nurses who came twice a day. When the nurses wanted to start morphine injections to treat Kate's pain, Rufus resisted strongly, because he knew Kate didn't like drugs. He also thought she would want to feel her pain and be aware of her departure, which to me seemed a little cruel. But at last the palliative care people persuaded Rufus that the kindest, best thing to do was to give her the morphine. Two days later, she fell into a coma state. And that's when Rufus called. I didn't have to come, he said, but if I wanted to, I should come right away. I left Brad and Arc in the park and ran back to the flat and booked a ticket home.

I arrived in Montreal at 2 a.m. Jörn, Rufus's partner, picked me up at the airport and told me Kate was still alive. When I came into her room, she made a noise, a small groan, which I found out later she hadn't done for a day or so. I think she knew I was there. I hope to god she knew I was there. Everyone left, and someone closed the door to give us some privacy.

I lay down next to her, and I pulled down her sheets to look at as much of her as possible. I kissed her everywhere I could. Her mouth was parted and dry, and there was a wet sponge on her bedside to wet her lips and mouth. I talked to her about the baby, and I apologized for all the pain I'd caused her. Eventually I fell asleep.

The next morning, Kate was still alive, and a steady stream of people came to pay their respects. Chaim, Emmylou, and all my mother's Montreal friends, and Loudon, too, who had been playing a few nearby gigs with Chaim and could now support Rufus by being there. It was like a dream in which the important people in your life are all in the same room, completely natural but also surreal, as if at any moment Gaby would also walk in and Frank, my mom's dad, was sitting whittling wood in the corner. They drank tea or wine and spoke in her presence, presumably at her and to her, but also about their own future plans. Could she hear them? Was this a kind of torture for her?

Or maybe she wasn't aware of them. I had such a short time with her. Brad and Arc had gone to stay with Linda Thompson while I was gone and would soon be running out of frozen breast milk. My flight was leaving that afternoon.

At some point that morning, Rufus and I both drew our mother in pencil. Rufus's drawings were better, but mine still caught her likeness. I sang her the lullabies she used to sing me and held her hand. Dr. Tabah was there with us, and a couple of times he came to Kate to smell her breath. From the smell, he could tell she was very close. She made some more groaning noises, and I became extremely fitful myself, almost as if I could feel her frustration. I kept crying out, "I'm sorry, I'm sorry, I'm so sorry." I was sorry that I had to go. I was sorry for everything. Mainly for not being there for her in her last few months. I was sorry for being a disappointment. For wasting my time. For being mediocre. For failing to carry a child to term. For not being smart. For not being everything she wanted me to be. But mostly I was sorry she was dying. I was sorry for her because I knew she must be afraid. Terrified. Angry. I wanted to say, "It's okay, it's okay, it's okay," but I couldn't because it wasn't. Nothing was okay; it was simply awful and wrong and unfair and seemed like the work of an unjust and cruel god. But that's not what it was. It was just death.

Then it was time to leave her. I didn't want to go but I was needed in London.

Kate was still alive when I boarded the plane. Luckily, the flight was empty and I found a whole row at the back. I downed a couple of bottles of plane wine, and then expressed with a hand pump right there in my seat with a scarf barely covering myself because I didn't fucking care if anyone saw, dumped the milk in the sink, and then lay down and fell asleep.

When I arrived at Linda's, she took me in her arms at the door and told me that Kate was gone. She led me to her bedroom, where Brad handed me our baby to nurse. Well, at least I could keep one person alive. The three of us sat on the bed in silence.

Later, Anna described Kate's last few hours to me. People played music for her. Not a recording either. No, they sat there in her bedroom and played. Emmylou had sung "Love and Happiness" to her while I was there, which was moving, but after I left, a hootenanny practically transpired. Could our family and friends not resist the urge to perform? Or maybe it's just the way we communicate.

I think Kate was aware the whole time and could hear everyone. But was she up for an actual show? Did she really want my father, a man she was still angry at, sitting over her as she died a premature death? Knowing Kate, I can only imagine how infuriating this would have been for her. Kate, who always loved to participate. Who always liked having the last word. Who always wanted to wow everyone with her great talent and charm. What a nightmare for her.

Anna felt this, too, I think, and was maddened by the spectacle of this poor woman trying to die with all these people singing at her. Asking her for attention. At last, Anna brought Kate's computer into the room and opened it up to Kate's iTunes. "I know what will release her," she said, her anxious voice and small frame cutting space in the room. And she played a recording of Kate, Rufus, and me from when Rufus and I were eight and five, singing a Christmas song called *"D'où viens-tu, bergère?"* or "Where Do You Come From, Shepherd?" Kate is playing the piano. In my five-year-old voice, I sing, *"D'où viens-tu, bergère?"* and Rufus replies, already so vocally strong, "I come from the manger, where I saw a miracle." Then I sing, *"Qu'as-tu vu, bergère?"* ("What did you see, shepherd?") and Rufus sings back that he saw Mother Mary giving the baby milk. My mother then joins in with me to sing, "Was He beautiful, shepherd?" and Rufus replies, softly and simply, that, yes, he was the most beautiful thing you'll ever see.

And with that, my mother died. It was on January 18, 2010, Arc's original due date.

Kate had galloped through her life, leaving an indelible trail. The impact of her death was just as indelible. Though we knew it was coming, nothing prepared us for her absence. Since her own mother had died at ninety-one, I think she had envisaged herself growing old, with her grandchildren around her, and becoming a sage of sorts. Until she was diagnosed and began to cut her losses. I had pictured her growing old in much the same way as she had always lived—avidly reading, doing her incredible knitting, traveling extensively, continuing to make records and to perform, continuing to write about Kerouac or on Greek mythology or whatever else sparked her prodigious curiosity. I always imagined that she would be here for a long time to help me in my life.

Cancer is strange. It doesn't discriminate. It's not judgmental but it is truly unjust. Before she got cancer, Kate mostly distanced herself from illness. She rarely went to the doctor and barely paid attention to her aging body. She didn't really have to. She was thin, active, and healthy. She slept well, and her mood was good. That she grew ill and died at sixty-three was strange, but the process of it all was filled with magic and mystery, too. To me, it felt as though a small light was passed between Kate and my son. As Arc grew stronger, Kate diminished, but for a time they danced together in the atmosphere of the earth and I believe she must have spoken to him in her dreams, trying to tell him as much as she could. Both gods and goblins seemed to be at work, making for emotional whirlwinds. Death is death, yes, but maybe because of Kate and who she was, or because of who we are as a family, to us she became like a demigod, living half in this world and half in the next.

Fifteen

Rufus agreed to wait until I could bring my family back to Montreal to have our mom's funeral, but I knew I couldn't make him wait too long. So I began my negotiations with the hospital. I wanted to get back as soon as possible to bury my mom, but I didn't want to kill my baby in the process. The doctors decided Arc could fly, but only with an oxygen supply. A regular tank was too much for a baby who weighed only six pounds, but the hospital had a machine that could step down the flow of oxygen, and the doctors bent the rules and loaned it to me. Still, they warned, if Arc were to stop breathing over the North Atlantic, I would have to keep him alive by manually pumping a little bag to deliver air into his lungs. I was so terrified of that possibility, I asked a family friend named Sonya, a neonatal nurse, to make a round trip to London so she could fly back with us. Lily came over to help, too; I needed her companionship and moral support. We would fly on January 29, with the wakes planned for January 30 and 31 at the funeral home at the top of Querbes on Laurier, and the service on February 1.

But before we left, we had to pack up the flat on Baker

Street because our lease was up. Rufus organized a place for us to stay, and we moved over to Sam Taylor-Wood's giant mansion on Primrose Hill for the remaining week or so while she was on holiday. Sam, a photographer, film-maker, and artist, was also the ex-wife of Jay Jopling, founder of the White Cube galleries, and her home was filled with works by the famous British artists. In my Marks & Spencer granny nightie, I carried the baby around from giant room to giant room in a haze of sadness while Brad played the Steinway under a neon Tracey Emin. Every now and then, I'd stop to stare out the giant picture windows that looked on Primrose Hill or to sink into one of the giant velvet couches.

When we arrived at Heathrow, we turned a lot of heads. What with all the stuff I'd bought—towels, sheets, baby bottles, a pump, even a carpet—we had a lot of big, heavy bags with us, more like we were making a covered-wagon crossing than an airplane flight. There were six of us in our party: me, Arc, Brad, Lily, Sonya, and Barbara Charone, who was coming for the funeral. We also had the special oxygen tank and a paramedic whose job was to get us on the plane and Arc settled in with the oxygen. Brad and I flew business, because I wanted the space. Lily and Sonya were supposed to fly coach, but Barbara had platinum status on British Airways and got them bumped up to business with the rest of us.

Brad was so happy to be leaving London that he, along with

Lily, began to drink in the lounge before the flight. We were allowed to board first to give the paramedic time to get Arc's machine working. As the other passengers passed by on the way to their seats, they looked appalled at the sight of such a little baby, but I just held him and nursed him and tried to keep calm. After we took off, Brad and Lily got more drinks. The stress of the whole situation had so overwhelmed Brad that now he wanted to cut loose, and soon he was pounding them down. Barbara had a couple, too, and everyone was happy and sad at the same time. But three-quarters of the way through the flight, Brad was getting a little out of hand, standing up and getting loud, I guess pretty excited to be getting out of London, and soon the flight attendants stopped serving him, and Lily too. Though they were nice about it. They could see the pain he was in.

Then Lily and Brad broke open their own duty-free booze, and that's when I got pissed off. We still had to land and go through Canadian customs and immigration with a newborn hooked up to an oxygen tank and an American father who was clearly drunk. By the time we got off the plane, Brad was swaying with the oxygen tank, which he dropped several times. I could have killed him. When we were through and had reclaimed our many bags, I refused to ride in the car with Brad.

Also, there was the fact that Kate was not at the airport to greet me. I knew she wouldn't be, and she had been too sick the last two times I'd landed in Montreal to come, but it still hit me like a ton of bricks that she was gone.

* * *

The apartment on Querbes looked beautiful. My cousins and some of Kate's old friends had really done it up, scrubbing it down and filling it with flowers as well as an old bassinet courtesy of Deborah the dancer, which had been passed down through generations of her family. It was freezing outside, minus 20 degrees Celsius, but the heat was jacked up—the first breaking of Kate's rule that if we were cold, we had to put on a sweater—and the apartment felt very cozy. The top of the piano was filled with condolence cards, and there were lots of soft chairs to sit in and pots of tea to drink. It was exactly what I wanted and needed—except for the thing I wanted and needed most. She must just be upstairs running a brush through her hair quickly and turning off the stove before flying down the stairs to hold her grandson and then look up at me with the biggest smile ever.

A succession of visitors came to see Arc. He was the firstborn grandchild on the Wainwright side, so aunts and uncles and cousins from my father's side of the family, all there for Kate's funeral, lined up to hold him. My mother-in-law, Marion, came, too. Neither Anna nor Marion thought I should bring the baby to the wakes and the funeral, and I was angry about that because I wanted the two to meet again. The ridiculousness of that idea finally sank in and I handed over the baby to Marion, who had offered to stay with him. Without the baby, I felt vulnerable and crazy. Without the baby, I was a child who had lost her mother.

In the years since Kate died, Rufus and I have spoken a

lot about Mom and how different his relationship with her was from mine. Rufus had always glorified her, and he became angry with Kate when she got sick, like he was somehow the victim of her shortened life. I had always mistrusted and resisted her on some level, but when I knew she was going to die, I began to adore her the way a small child adores her mother. I hadn't fully appreciated her until then, whereas only now was Rufus able to see any of her faults. He told me that at one point when he was taking care of her in her final weeks, he had to leave to do a couple of shows, which he'd asked Lucy to open for him. Kate gave him a hard time about it, and he was pissed. Kate had never been able to accept our half sister Lucy, something that made both me and Rufus sad. Since Kate's death, Lucy and I have become even closer, no doubt partially because my mother isn't here.

Anna insists that Rufus and I were the most important things in my mother's life, and that Kate viewed us as her greatest accomplishment. I'm not so sure about this, but I understand why Anna would think it. Kate was an angry child and, later, a disappointed wife. She wanted to be famous, much more than Anna ever did, but she wasn't able to branch out on her own. She and Anna both fell into domesticity, neglecting their natural state, which was to be artistic misfits.

I'm not sad my mother made that choice—how could I be?—but I wonder if she had regrets. Anna likes to tell the story of when she and Kate got a call on that old phone at St. Sauveur from the secretary at Le Studio, at the time a famous recording studio that was just a couple of miles up the road. The Police were making their album *Synchronicity* there and wanted Kate and Anna to come hang out and possibly... god knows what, sing or schmooze or both. Anna told the secretary that she'd just popped a chicken in the oven so she couldn't make it. Or maybe it was Mark Knopfler, not the Police, but whoever it was, she was proud of turning these people down. I think Kate would have preferred to go, but they were a duo and Kate always took her cues from her older sister.

For her part, when Kate died, Anna lost a piece of herself. No one understood and knew Kate as much as Anna. She was the first to say how remarkable her sister was. Anna also said that because Kate never got to go as far as she wanted in music, she lived vicariously through Rufus and me as we tried to realize our own dreams. When she had us, she found something to focus on and protect, which helped her in life in some ways. But she also made the choice that many women are forced to make, putting her kids before her work.

Not surprisingly, Rufus wanted to go big for Kate's funeral. It was held at Notre-Dame Basilica, the largest Catholic cathedral in Montreal, modeled after its namesake in Paris down to the flying buttresses. Now that Kate was gone, Rufus wanted the world to acknowledge and remember her and the McGarrigles.

The last time our family had come together like this was at my wedding, and though Kate's funeral was a somber occasion, there was also an undeniable feeling of warmth and celebration and love about it. Especially at the wakes, where we passed around mickeys of whiskey and told funny stories. Weird things happen at wakes, most likely because wakes are weird.

And speaking of weird, I had wanted an open casket, perhaps because I didn't get to see my mom die. When I was small, I remember having powerful experiences at my great-uncle Lorne's funeral and, later, at my grandmother's wake. In both instances, I was compelled to touch them and found it both moving and helpful. My mother had talked about stealing into the town morgue as a kid to touch the local people there, some of whom she must have known. Bodies are just the framework, the container, but they are also what is left, and you want to say goodbye to that, too. To me, when the coffin is closed, the person seems so stuck. Also, my mother was beautiful and still relatively young when she died, and her physical being was a huge part of who she was as a performer. I thought she would want to be displayed.

Anna was not happy about the idea, though. And it was certainly a little macabre considering that Kate had died almost two weeks earlier. So, to make sure we were okay with the open-casket idea, Rufus and I went to the funeral home to check it out before people started to arrive.

Well, the person in the casket didn't look like Kate, and soon Rufus and I started futzing around with the undertaker's work. Anna had given the dresser mittens to put on Kate, but Rufus thought they were all wrong. When he started to pull them off, though, he realized that the orangey makeup she was covered in hadn't made it onto her hands, which were snow white. For

191

some reason, Kate also was wearing a woolly hat, but when we tried to get rid of that, we found it was sewn on. Her chest was inflated and rounded as if she had literally been stuffed. Her lips looked thinner than usual and had been painted a strange coral color. Being halfway out of my mind, I asked the first of the women arriving for the wake to show me their lipsticks. I found one that was darker, with a little more purple in it, that I felt would suit Kate better and borrowed it. I then went back to Kate, wiped off what had been applied, and overlaid her lips with this new darker color, leaning so far I was practically in the coffin. I remember that all the while I was laughing, but I was also serious about getting it right.

I found out that making up a dead face is like trying to put makeup on a rock. The skin doesn't move, and nothing sticks. I managed to ruin her makeup quite profoundly, giving her a smeared lipstick line that made her look like she was smiling. I returned the lipstick to whoever had loaned it to me—I can't remember if I confessed what I had been doing with it, but I hope so—and went into the corridor and began bawling. On the second day of the wake, we closed the casket.

Despite it being a freezing day, the funeral was well attended. There were a bunch of camera crews and journalists outside the big church, so it made the evening news. I wore my mother's clothes to her funeral: a black wool dress and colorful Paul Smith tights that expressed her sensibility, and usually my own but not on this day. I know I gave a eulogy, but I can't remember what I said. I lost the only copy I had when I was mugged a couple of years later and the thieves stole my laptop.

After the funeral, Brad returned to New York, desperate to get home and back to his life, while I stayed on with Arc in Canada for a few weeks. I needed my family around me, and then there were all the loose ends that needed tying up. But Kate's lifetime of stuff—the colorful costumes and abandoned instruments crying to be played, the handwritten notes and meaningful pictures, everything that was in the closets—would have to wait. I didn't have it in me.

Sixteen

THE VACUUM THAT WAS CREATED by Kate's departure was filled by a few people, but mainly by my aunt Teddy, my father's sister, who became a second mother to Rufus and me.

She came to Montreal a few weeks before Kate died because Rufus asked for her help. He was staying with Kate, but he was finding it overwhelming. Kate's sisters were also overwhelmed; having been there for every twist and turn of the three or more years of my mom's illness, this last stage was almost too much for them. Teddy herself was deeply lost, but she was also searching for something to keep her alive. In 2005, her only child, Jack, had died a tragic death at nineteen. He had taken too many pills, fallen asleep with a lit cigarette, and died of smoke inhalation. She found him in his apartment. Since then she had been on a death march, blowing through her savings, drinking heavily, traveling around aimlessly or sitting in her armchair for hours, desperately trying to find a reason to go on living.

Teddy's actual name was Martha, like mine. It was her mother's name, but she never went by it. She wasn't that close to her mom, or I should say her mother wasn't that close to her. Martha, my grandmother, doted on Loudon and left Teddy to her own devices. I don't know firsthand what the dynamic was, but from my point of view, Teddy was the victim of one of those family injustices. If she had been a man, she could have become president of anything, but as a woman, she believed she was unsuccessful, even though she was brilliant, an avid reader, a hard (if fitful) worker, funny and popular outside her immediate family. She also had a hard time rising above her conception of herself as plain. She was overweight, and she gravitated toward drugs and alcohol, and being as strong as an ox, she could take her self-destructive tendencies a long way. My dad was hard on her and had little patience for her imperfections. I know he made her feel insecure. I'm sure he had his reasons, given that Teddy was complicated. No one looked down on her more than she did herself.

No one else could have helped Rufus and me as much as she did. She understood the pain we were feeling intimately, and held our hands through the sad, drawn-out process of closing up Kate's life on earth. Teddy had spent years taking care of others, and selflessly. She had managed her brother's career for almost twenty years, and also the Roches'. With her sister, Sloan, she had run the very successful Baker's Cafe in Katonah, New York. She had dedicated herself to bringing up Jack, who had learning differences, caring for him with intense love and working tirelessly to find him tutors, speech therapists, and specialists. When her best friend and her best friend's husband both died of cancer a couple of years apart, she became the guardian of their two teenage kids. And now Rufus and I needed her more than we even realized.

In the months and years after Kate's passing, Teddy not only became our primary parent, she also managed our separate careers, which were very active at the time, dealing with the labels, agents, lawyers, and musicians. She became the producer for a formidable run of musical tributes to Kate and the family Christmas concerts that would run for another ten years. She came on tour with both of us and dealt with most of the tedious and clerical tasks that neither one of us is good at. She also took care of our kids as needed and helped us through our complicated and strange family lives. For instance, after Rufus and Lorca Cohen had a child together in 2011, a daughter they called Viva, their parental relationship quickly became extremely complicated. Rufus and Lorca had been very close friends, but having a kid together ruptured their friendship completely, as well as mine with Lorca. She wanted to have a child essentially on her own, but Rufus wanted to be more involved. They had not straightened this out clearly enough at the beginning, I guess, and there ensued a serious power struggle and then a custody dispute. It was extremely emotional, painful, and hard to watch, as these things often are. When Rufus married his partner, Jörn Weisbrodt, in 2012, Teddy oversaw much of the wedding, which was designed to solidify not only their deep emotional bond but also their work relationship; Rufus and Jörn adore each other, but they are a power couple, too. They also wanted to get married simply to affirm their right to do so as a gay couple. The ceremony was a snapshot of the world of opera management and performance art, with many movers and shakers in the art world attending. Jörn had been the American experimental director and playwright Robert Wilson's assistant and then the director of Wilson's Watermill performance lab on Long Island for years, and had also run the Berlin State Opera; he was about to become the head of Toronto's Luminato arts festival.

Like my wedding, it was big and involved and took a lot of planning, and Teddy organized a lot of it, under some pressure to make sure it was a better event than mine (Rufus and I are still competitive about some things). Instead of St. Sauveur, the venue was Montauk, Long Island, and all that comes with that. A certain privilege, a few more famous people in attendance than at mine (but not that many more), the ocean, and the money. Weddings can be so dramatic. I remember struggling to learn the bridge on "How Deep Is the Ocean," which I was to sing with a quartet for the ceremony. I also remember that Lorca was pissed off to be there and lawyers were chasing after Jörn to sign a prenup until minutes before the ceremony, and many of the participants were struggling not to drink too much, too fast. But Jörn and Rufus were sure of what they were doing, and that felt good to watch. The wedding ended with a fire on the beach, nudity, a last swim, and Mark Ronson serenading us on the guitar. I personally think my wedding might have been better after all, but my brother's marriage proved to be the better one.

Teddy knew every date in our calendars, whether it was for

a big TV performance or a dentist appointment. She knew the contents of our bank accounts and what we were paying people or getting paid ourselves. She knew our kids' teachers and their school friends by name. She was part fairy godmother and part personal secretary, and she became our rock.

Though I had wanted to have my baby near my family in Montreal, the deal with Brad was that our home base would continue to be New York. Before we'd left on the trip to England where Arc was born, we'd closed on buying a big brownstone on Greene Avenue in BedStuy in Brooklyn. After I had done what I could with Teddy and Rufus to settle Kate's affairs, we moved into our new place to begin a new chapter in our lives, bringing all the baggage of the past, along with much of the furniture from the triplex on Querbes, to try to fill this giant of a house.

The place resembled the house in Westmount where I'd grown up, but it needed so much repair and was in a rough neighborhood, so it fit both the intensity of the emotional situation and my reputation for doing things the hard way. Turning it into a home felt downright daunting. There were beautiful and soft things around us—hand-knitted baby blankets and other gifts for the new motherless mother and homeowner—but underneath our situation there was tension and fear and sadness that couldn't be denied.

I tried to bring my family together. I put photos of us up on the walls, the way I'd seen done in other homes. I invited people for Sunday dinners, members of my family and Brad's family—a vinaigrette of personalities. I did what I could to welcome everyone from the fragmented broken homes of our lives, all the steps and halfs and in-laws, some of whom felt like they were from another planet. Armed with my apron and wooden spoon, I served them wine and roast dinners and tried to make everything all right on Greene Avenue.

Brad and I had put every penny we had into buying this house (and eventually rented a first-floor flat and some rooms upstairs to friends to keep up with the mortgage payments). Wanting to do some of the work himself, Brad bought a toolbox and proceeded to lower the property value. I carefully talked him down off the ladder and took the paintbrush out of his hand and hired friends who knew what they were doing. Phil, along with a friend, redid the old bathroom and the kitchen, and when he was finished, I felt very grown-up in my refurbished house. I kitted Arc's room out with beautiful toys and wonderful books and spent hours on the floor with him, trying different techniques to get him to roll over or hold his head up during tummy time. He was an easy and charming baby, and Brad and I reveled in his presence. He was hitting the milestones, always a worry after a birth like his, but a little late. I read books on child development and, following the experts' advice, I tried to get him to sleep in his crib, rather than in bed with us. Never happened. Only laundry ever slept there.

I wanted so much to enjoy this time with my baby, and I did, but when the sun went down, Kate's loss was everywhere, and my tears would come. I realized that it was time to work, and not only for financial reasons. We went back out on the road to promote the Piaf album.

Arc's first tour started in Istanbul when he was only five months old. Teddy came along to act as his nanny, and she and I pushed Arc in the stroller through the bazaars and mosques of the ancient city. Over the next year, Arc crawled and then learned to walk in the great parks of Europe, in the shadow of the Sydney Opera House, and in late-night bistros in Paris. There were a few grungy backstages, too, but by the time he was two, he had sung with me at Carnegie Hall and the Royal Albert and many more of the greatest stages on earth.

I realize now that I was so focused on Arc and my music and the house and myself that my marriage was deteriorating before my eyes. I would traipse around the city with my son, going on little adventures or visiting friends. I would often go on the road alone with Arc or take him up to Montreal while Brad would stay in Brooklyn, working in his studio, or he'd be on tour with someone else. I did bring up the state of things between us with Brad, even suggesting that we separate, but every time I raised our situation, he got angry and shut the conversation down. I was still blanketed in the sadness of losing Kate. Brad, too, was very sad about Kate. Often, he would talk about how wrecked he was by her death, and he seemed almost jealous of the condolences I received. Or he felt that there wasn't enough room for him and how he felt about it—that his grief was being ignored.

Where we still could connect to each other, and where Brad maybe best connected with people, was through music.

In 2010 and 2011, we did three tribute concerts dedicated to Kate and recorded them all to make an album produced by Joe Boyd and a documentary called *Sing Me the Songs That Say I Love You: A Concert for Kate McGarrigle*, directed by Lian Lunson (who had made *Leonard Cohen: I'm Your Man*). The first one was at Royal Festival Hall in London and is a bit of a blur, to be honest. What I remember, though, is how it helped me come to a full realization of who Kate was as an artist. Of course, I knew her songs and had sung with her plenty of times, but now I had to sing her parts. Now I had to really pay attention. Now I had to know all the words. I couldn't lean on her anymore.

I used to lose my voice all the time. And when I lost it onstage and my mother was there, I would look at her and say "Help me" with my eyes and she would step in to sing my part. Now I couldn't lose my voice without being exposed. I had to be the adult. I was thirty-three, a new mom, and a grieving daughter, and, with Rufus, I finally had to learn how to run the show.

And we did it, each in our own way: reunified and fortified, the bond between a brother and a sister brought together by grief and a need for the other's talent, personality, and understanding. Mom, Rufus, and I had been a very tight unit. First with Pat, our stepdad, and then without him. Now Rufus and I made a new family, and with our partners and our kids and Teddy, we created a new family ship that we sailed through the music business, trying to keep afloat, trying to leave a mark, trying to make money for the Kate McGarrigle Foundation— and at least cover our costs.

These concerts, the Kate tributes and the Christmas performances, were also where and when we saw each other and the
rest of the circus. Anna and Janie and their kids, our cousins,
would be onstage singing, as well as backstage designing merch
to sell and moving instruments and organizing rehearsals.
Rufus and I also wanted the Wainwrights to be part of these
shows, and Lucy, Sloan, and our dad (somewhat begrudgingly
but always with great results) now participated regularly. Each
singer was there to support the group as well as to stand out
and leave an impression. Rufus and I were definitely stage hogs,
although Dad came close, wanting to make sure that he was
regarded as the sort of patriarch. Rufus and I accommodated
him but, just as we had when we were kids, we often rolled
our eyes at his song choices or his lack of enthusiasm. But
the audiences always liked what he did, so I guess he showed
us he really was the patriarch. Fathers, they always make sure
they're felt.

Many of the musicians had been part of it all since
Kate and Anna had begun the concerts, and would return
year after year, whether we were in New York or Montreal,
London, Los Angeles, Nashville, San Francisco, Toronto, or
Dublin. (Just thinking about these places as I sit here in my
COVID seclusion, I am desperate to travel again.) And then
there were the guest artists we asked to join us depending
on that year's location. In New York, Laurie Anderson and
Lou Reed, Justin Vivian Bond, Anohni, Cyndi Lauper, Hal
Willner, Jimmy Fallon, Cibo Matto, Sean Lennon, Norah
Jones. In London, Guy Garvey; Boy George; Richard and

Linda Thompson and their kids, Teddy and Kami; Neil Tennant from the Pet Shop Boys; and Chrissie Hynde. In LA, Carrie Fisher, Maria Muldaur and her daughter Jenni, Van Dyke Parks. In Nashville, Emmylou, of course, and Alison Krauss, Jamey Johnson, Karen Elson, Chris Stills. And in Montreal and Toronto, Robert Charlebois, Michel Rivard, Ariane Moffatt, Elisapie, Patrick Watson, Broken Social Scene, Mary Margaret O'Hara, and . . . you get the idea. A lot of great artists.

Some of the many standout moments: Laurie Anderson singing "Little Town of Bethlehem" through a vocoder that brought her voice down an octave. Lou calmly thrashing out a version of "Mother" on the guitar, with Sean Lennon on the piano. Me getting the chance to sing a duet of "Silver Bells" with Alison Krauss in Nashville, Renée Fleming in NYC, and Martha Plimpton and Lucy in London. Rufus bringing the house to their feet every goddamn time with a sans-amplification version of "O Holy Night." Me and Jimmy Fallon flirting our way through "Baby, It's Cold Outside," before we had to stop singing that song. Hal Willner and Justin Vivian Bond making us think a little more than we were used to, riffing on the ridiculousness of Christmas and the tragicomedy of humanity. And then, perhaps the best, the poignant and tremendous finale, "Proserpina," sung by Anna, Rufus, Sloan, and myself, along with everyone else in the show, all of us onstage.

Still, working with family can be hard. The concerts amplified family dynamics and insecurities; there was bickering and often tears. I often argued with Brad, who was usually leading the six-piece band along with Thomas Bartlett and Doug Wieselman. These fights with Brad caused a lot of stress, but he was a part of the family and we all got used to the friction. Rufus and I also argued a lot, but it made us closer. The music brought us into our emotions but also protected us from them. The after-parties were often epic, filled with regrettable moments and followed by terrible hangovers. At least for me. Have I mentioned that Rufus doesn't drink or do drugs anymore? I envy him for that. Sometimes.

Seventeen

UNEXPECTEDLY, WHEN ARC WAS ONLY one, I got pregnant again. My instinct is always just to roll with the punches, and I also love babies, so once I was over the initial shock, I was happy about it. Brad wasn't so happy, telling me he didn't want another child. I found a doctor in Montreal, because once again that is where I wanted to have the baby. When I went for the first ultrasound, I found out I was carrying twins. That frightened me, and really upset Brad. Though he is a twin himself, he was very concerned about having three kids under the age of two—he wanted to concentrate on his music, not have all these kids. Then I began to worry that since Arc came early, the twins would, too. I knew if that happened, Brad would blame me, as he had for Arc's premature birth. Although Arc was born two weeks after the flight to London, Brad believed that I should never have gotten on the plane. Or that if I had been followed by a doctor, not a midwife, the crisis wouldn't have happened. Or at least that is what I think he believed. He was never clear about exactly what I had done wrong, but he was sure that I had done something wrong.

I sought advice from friends and family about what I should

do. Some told me that whatever happens, you never regret having children. Others said that more babies would slow down my career, and for a long time. I became extremely sad. I visited doctors who said they could do a "reduction," which is when they terminate only one of the twins. The whole thing was crazy.

Finally, I decided I wanted to keep the babies, and Brad's response was that it was my body and that it was up to me. But I knew that he was not behind my decision, and I was worried about what he'd do if anything went wrong. Then he told me that if these babies were born early, he would never forgive me, and that was it: I couldn't go ahead with the pregnancy. Brad had said, over and over, that I needed to focus on Arc, who was still only a baby himself, and so I justified it to myself by saying that I needed to be able to work, too, to support us all. Two very good reasons. I thought, I'll take the conservative and careful option, rather than the emotional and potentially risky one that I usually opt for.

We needed to get on a plane for Australia to start a Piaf tour, and a friend arranged an appointment for me at a clinic there, which we'd be shuttled to as soon as we landed. I remember Arc slept the whole way from LA and Brad popped a couple of sleeping pills and calmly watched movies. I spent a lot of the flight crying. At one point, I said to him, "Have you made your peace with this? Have you said goodbye?" He didn't understand the notion, or that for me the babies were already so real. I'd had morning sickness and my stomach was growing bigger. For Brad, like many men, fatherhood only clicked when he could pick the baby up. I was so obviously devastated that in the clinic waiting room, Brad told me that we could leave. But I felt I had no choice but to go through with it.

After the abortion, I think I had a nervous breakdown. I felt such a deep sense of loss and despair, I began to mistrust Brad. To avoid my anger, he ended up spending more of his time with Thomas, who was on the road with us, than with me and Arc. At one point, I thought *they* were having an affair. I imagine my mind went there because I had always suspected Brad of infidelity. Things were out of focus, not just the backdrop of weird Australian animals and primordial-looking forests and the night sky I didn't recognize, but everything. The fact that I was thousands of miles from home upset me where it usually exhilarated me. I saw shadows that I thought were Kate. I sang like a wild woman, throwing myself into the performances, and medicated myself with giant glasses of Australian Shiraz.

I was miserable for weeks, clinging to Arcangelo. At last, I was able to say goodbye to my lost ones, but I also got down on my knees and asked them for forgiveness. I told them I would come back for them. And I made Brad promise that one day we could try again.

With all the stress and lost souls, the flow of wine and tears, singing Piaf somewhat convincingly, which is exhausting, and losing connection to Brad, I started writing songs again.

I made my album *Come Home to Mama* with Yuka Honda from Cibo Matto, and it saved me. I was still miserable and angry and scared, but while I was making it, I felt protected and nurtured. I had told Brad that I couldn't deal with a male producer this time. I needed to make a record with a woman. He was the one who suggested Yuka, and I was glad that he did, and he was glad, too, because he could both take credit for the fact that he had suggested her and then shit on what he didn't like about the record.

But I didn't care. For three to four hours a couple of days a week, I would walk to Sean Lennon's house in town, where Yuka and her husband, Nels Cline, were living, and be the old me. Yuka did most of the work. I would come in and sing my vocals and then I would leave, and she would do overdubs and get Nels to add incredible guitar tracks.

Every time I arrived at the door of the four-story classic New York brownstone, Yuka would make me high-quality Japanese tea. Sometimes Yoko would be sitting in the little dark basement kitchen when we came in, poised in the corner like a queen, and she would say arresting and painful things like "We only live to die" in her sweet, but a little scary, Japanese-accented voice. There was a steady flow of young artists, hangers-on, supermodels, and famous or about-to-be-famous people, coming on or off hard drugs, and all around us were hundreds of guitars and amps, keyboards, paints and pencils, easels, signed artwork, swords, hats, costumes, bottles of wine, tinctures and tarot decks, little dogs and a snake.

Sean's girlfriend, a model who wore little to no clothing and read lots of poetry and painted, was completely sweet and charming. Sean, a talented musician and a super-funny guy, kept everyone entertained, except when he was fast asleep on the couch, exhausted from his countless artistic projects or just from the night before. It was a fun house, and although I mostly went there to work for a few daylight hours, I stumbled out of there well past dawn a few times. I did a lot of my vocals in a small closet, where I pushed aside jackets that looked an awful lot like those worn on the cover of *Sgt. Pepper's*. Could they be? Yes, they could.

I can never thank Yuka and Sean enough for that time we had together. I had been a fan of Yuka's since I was sixteen, and I was really moved by how well she treated me as a friend and as an artist. She would tell me that I was singing great that day or be very positive about my chord changes. I wasn't used to encouragement and praise. Maybe she was overly positive, but it felt good. And after my experience making the record with her, I understood that I needed to be around more people who were positive and good.

When we went out on the road next time, I invited Ariel and her husband, Andrew Whiteman, to join us. Andrew is the cofounder of Broken Social Scene. I asked if they could open the shows with their duo, AroarA, and then Andrew could also be the guitar player and Ariel could sing backup in my set. Ariel was already one of my best friends, and Andrew soon became another of them. Arc was two and a half and the cutest thing you could imagine. I hired a great drummer, Yuval Lyon, and his wife, a yoga teacher, also came out for some of the dates and helped with Arc. I thought it was wonderful to be on a tour bus in Europe, playing good shows to decent crowds, surrounded by people I loved. But Brad was not happy.

He didn't love the material from the new album, and he didn't love Andrew or Ariel.

Or maybe that's not true. I actually can't say why he was so angry, but he was. There were some lyrics in my new material that he didn't like. For instance, *I really like the make-up sex / It's the only kind I ever get.* And *My marriage is failing but I keep trying.* Or *The seven-year itch / Is quite a bitch.* But in every case, the overall message of the song is that marriage is hard but worth it and that love prevails. My lyrics were personal, yes, but that's the only way I know how to write songs. I thought the songs were positive, but from what I can tell, that's not how Brad heard or felt them. He also didn't like Yuka's arrangements and maybe he felt outnumbered with Andrew and Ariel along for this ride.

We started the tour in Oslo, and I bought a long wool skirt and a light-blue beaded sweater, which was my outfit for most of the tour. Brad felt the need to get his own outfit—a clown costume with a giant wig. When the bus driver threw out the wig by accident, Brad was incensed. He bought a monk's cloak and a scary mask to wear instead. Onstage, he would say disparaging things about me on the mic and push me to argue with him. It was sometimes so uncomfortable for the audience that people gasped and commented on social media. Brad and I had always done a "Take my wife, please" schtick that had been fun for us, but it wasn't fun anymore. I mostly shrugged it off because I didn't want to deal with it, and spent even more time with the band and with Arc.

No matter what he felt, *Come Home to Mama* wasn't about

Brad, it was about Kate. It was a way to keep her alive in music. The tribute shows were another way of keeping her music alive. Could I ever shake her ghost, let her rest in peace? Not quite, but I could learn from her, and that is what I tried to do.

Near the end of that tour, we flew again to Australia. It became a magical time in which Brad and I found some peace after the rocky trip through Europe. I told Brad it would be nice to conceive another child there, especially considering that we had left the two behind. I know that sounds sentimental and overly dramatic, but it was how I felt, and I managed to persuade him that it was fitting. I don't know if we would have lasted much longer as a couple if we hadn't.

With a new baby on the way, I also told Brad that it was time for us to go back to Montreal. I wanted the kids to know my aunts and cousins and for Arc to go to school in French. I wanted my children to have Canadian citizenship. But more than anything, I wanted to go home. I had left the house that I had inherited from my mother and now I needed to face what was in it.

Brad didn't really want to spend time in Montreal, but we had made a deal when we were married that we would live there for a while at some point and see how it went. Also, as I pointed out, my family and friend network there was extensive and would be a great help when we had two kids. And so we started to pack.

Eighteen

KATE ALWAYS USED TO MEET me at the airport when I came home, with arms flailing to get my attention.

Yes, I can see you, Mother.

Or, if I was making the long drive, she'd be there at home with dinner waiting in the oven. But now that she was gone, I would have to hail the taxi at the airport or pull the kids out of the back seat of the car in subzero temperatures myself. Fumble for the key and walk into a cold, dark, lonely house. Nobody would be there to welcome me—to welcome us—home.

Maybe that's why I wanted to come back to Montreal. Not to return to my dead mother's house, but to make a home for my new growing family in the place she'd left behind. To undo the bad with good. A fresh start in a familiar place.

My mother held on to everything, and there was even more memorabilia, or really just crap, from my tours and Rufus's. Fans' artworks and letters. Bags and bags of old clothes, furniture she filched from damp alleyways. Lots of scrap paper filled with lyrics of mine, or Rufus's, or Kate's own. Clippings of reviews and articles, record contracts, posters and flyers, makeup and hairpins, reading glasses from the pharmacy, old medications and soaps, broken lampshades, countless pencils and pens, and mounds of change in multiple currencies. I had to go through all of it, but being a nostalgic person, I lacked the instinct to throw things out. Lily and Sylvan and Aunt Jane's son, my wonderful cousin Vinnie, and his partner, Kathleen, helped a lot, clearing and cleaning and painting and doing. Kathleen's parents had been best friends with my mom when they were all growing up, and now she was with my cousin; she took real care of Arc and me. These were people I had spent my childhood and teenage years with—we were like a pack. In the evenings, we'd sit around and watch hockey (something I'd never done) or the news and sort through another layer of Kate's stuff. We laughed so much as we reminisced, it hurt our stomachs. It was a real homecoming—we reconnected and fused together like we had when we were kids, and I felt safe and happy and protected from bad things. Brad liked them all, too.

He had stayed in New York to work on a record while the renovations were being done in Montreal; to accommodate our family, we were creating a duplex from the triplex, joining the ground-floor and second-floor apartments on Querbes. I found Arc a spot at a day care, and he and I couch surfed while walls were being knocked out and staircases rebuilt. We stayed for a while with Ariel and Andrew. She was pregnant, too, just a month ahead of me. Anna had her city pied-à-terre down the block and sometimes we would stay there, too. It was both deeply familiar and felt like a new beginning. Every night, Arc and I talked about the baby in Mommy's tummy.

We pretended the baby was a baby deer and I was the mommy deer and Arc was the daddy deer. These are the little things that make you happy.

The winter Francis was born was one of the coldest in a long time, way down in the minus-twenties for weeks at a time. By then, we were able to live at Querbes, and I remember covering all the windows in plastic and plugging any holes around doorframes that could let the cold in. I was heavily pregnant and joyfully uncomfortable; I'd never gotten to look and feel so pregnant with Arc. It was hard to sleep, though. I'd often wake up at 3 or 4 a.m. and make tea and just start my day. I was so relieved that this baby would not be born premature—that I was not a failure.

Brad was still mostly in New York as my cousins and I put the finishing touches on the place. Hanging a chandelier and putting up towel racks. Washing everything, putting plates and cups away in the cupboards, and endlessly, happily, wiping the construction dust away. Brad came up for good the last month before I was due. He was excited about the baby, but not in the way that I was. Montreal grated on him. He made fun of the French Canadian accent and bitched about the cold. When he compared Montreal to New York unfavorably, my cousins and I laughed and rolled our eyes. We made warm stews and nibbled on crusty bread we'd buy at the corner.

I hoped Brad might soften. Though things were strained between us, I wanted it to work. I also felt I had no choice but to make it work. Before we got married, Brad had made it clear that as far as he was concerned, marriage vows were for life.

At around three in the morning of February 5, 2014, I started leaking amniotic fluid. I woke Brad and told him I was going to take a cab to the hospital to find out if I was in labor, and that he needed to stay with Arc and get him to prekindergarten in the morning.

I was scared, but mostly thrilled. I felt like a big fat princess. Again, I hadn't wanted to know the sex. Frances was Kate's middle name, after her father, Francis, and I liked it. I also liked Winnie, Wendy, Mona-Lisa, Fern, Gold, and Proserpina, or Pina for short. For a boy, other than Francis, I liked Jules, Valentine, and Winter.

By the time I got to the hospital, I was having contractions. My doctor wasn't on call, which meant that another doctor would perform my surgery. I met with the new ob-gyn and we went over what was going to happen. In the event that something went wrong, she asked if I was prepared for her to perform a hysterectomy or did I want her to try to save my uterus. I told her I wanted her to do whatever she needed to do to deliver the baby safely, and if that meant a hysterectomy, fine. Her question surprised me, but it was good to be reminded of the seriousness of the situation and that the best outcome was baby and mother both alive. We had to hurry, though, because I was in labor, which makes the procedure harder. Then I started to get scared, thinking about the needle in my spine and the pain that would follow the operation. I reminded myself of how

I'd pushed away all fear the last time I was in this situation. I hadn't had the luxury of thinking of myself because the baby, and Kate's life, were in the balance.

Brad arrived at the hospital with Anna about then, and instead of looking handsome to me in his scrubs, he was so chipper and talkative he was getting on my nerves. I wanted quiet. With my contractions five minutes apart, they wheeled me into the operating room. The environment was relaxed, even joyful. (It's easy sometimes to forget how routine giving birth is, but also how gruesome.) The anesthesiologist asked what I did for a living. I told him I was a singer and he asked me my name, then said he had heard of Rufus. Typical! But he had his phone with him, and he googled me. The first thing that came up was a video I had made of "Proserpina." He pressed the Play button and the song suddenly filled the room.

I was slightly embarrassed to hear my own voice, but mostly I was moved. To have Kate there with me was special, especially since that song had become one of the ones most associated with her since her death. The anesthesiologist asked me about my mom and I told him she had died four years earlier after a long battle with cancer, much of it spent in this very hospital. Then and there I decided that if the baby was a girl, we would name her Proserpina.

But instead of a little girl, I had another son, Francis Valentine, who came into the world that snowy February morning. A large and wonderful baby, even though he, too, was early, born at thirty-six weeks. He would have been huge if he had gone full-term. In fact, the doctors wouldn't have allowed me to carry him to full term, because if you have had the classical procedure, they make sure they deliver the next one before your due date.

I loved having two kids. I loved nursing Francis and also taking care of Arc.

At one point that winter, when Francis was maybe two months old, Brad was away working and I was alone with the kids for a week. Arc had scarlet fever. I would lie nursing Francis in my big bed, and then I would hear Arc call for me from his room. I would run to lie with him and put cold cloths on his brow, staying until the baby started crying again and I'd have to tell Arc I'd be right back. I needed to keep the kids separate, and it was such a juggle, but Arc was patient and understanding and eventually everyone slept. I'd never felt so useful. So valid. So important. So needed. In those days of my marriage, I was sometimes left alone with the kids while Brad toured or went to New York City for work. In a way, it was easier. No arguments. One person in charge.

Francis was a joy. A super-easy, happy baby. He slept well and ate well and brought calm to the house. In stark contrast to Arc, there was no stress around Francis's developmental milestones and general health. I felt extremely close to him, of course, but the bond that really surprised me was the one that grew between the brothers. Arcangelo was very sweet and gentle with Francis, and Francis adored him. It was moving to watch.

It made sense to stay on in Montreal where we could lean on my aunts and my cousins. Arc had all his specialists at the hospital: the cardiologist to monitor the holes in his heart, which eventually closed; the neurologist we consulted for the developmental and learning differences that eventually came to light; the orthopedic surgeon. The schools were great, free, and close by. We started making new friends to add to my old ones. But even as we grew more settled, Brad felt more isolated. He complained relentlessly about the French and the cold, even the lack of good pizza. I encouraged him to go to New York to work more regularly and to see his family, but he didn't want to be pushed out, as he saw it. He was torn: he wanted to work and to be free to move around, but he did not want to be told that he should do it. He became more low. His mother came for visits, but she didn't like Montreal either. It was not her turf. People could see his frustration and they would make the obvious suggestions that I was also making, but he didn't seem to want to take anyone's advice.

I'm still not sure exactly why Brad clung so hard to our marriage. His own parents had been divorced when he was five. I and many of our friends were from so-called broken homes. He married late and maybe reluctantly, but once we'd said our vows, he told me that he was never going to do what his dad had done and get a divorce. Is this what arrested development looks like? Was some part of him still a five-year-old who felt abandoned? I was a child of divorce, too, but I never believed my marriage *had* to last forever. What I'd whispered to myself before our wedding came back to haunt me then—*I can always get a divorce*. Eight years later, nothing about getting a divorce looked easy.

Still, I truly believe that both Brad and I wanted to stay together, perhaps just to prove that we could. For two years after Francis was born, we tried. We went to counseling and talked to our friends and family, but in the end, after a succession of painful and dramatic events, our marriage had to end. His dogged insistence on sticking to our vows forced me to be the one who "left," as if I was guilty of something when it was quite the opposite. I'm going to leave it at that, because to get into those events would drag us down into a tawdry, depressing, pointless place.

I knew that it would be best for the children, and myself, to break it off with Brad. Still, I was not prepared for the repercussions that a very bad divorce would have.

My dream in life was to be a mother and a singer—to be able to do both equally well. It's not common. The careers of many female artists slow down or come to a screeching halt after they've had kids, like my mother's did. There are very few role models of woman artists, singers in particular, who are also considered good, or even just acceptable, parents. Woman singers who choose to keep working are often depicted as damaged and selfish mothers—think of Nina Simone or Judy Garland. But I was going to be different.

I'd pictured Brad and me and the kids on the road as a family, and we did get to do a little of that. After the separation, I thought that I would still be able to travel with the kids or leave them with their father for short stints while I did shows and then come back to the kids and he would get to go out and work with other artists, as he had in the past. At one point, I even thought that after the dust had settled, Brad would come on tour sometimes, too—that we'd pass through our troubles and come out the other side as friends. I had it all pictured in my head, down to homeschooling Arc and Francis on the tour bus. We would run through the great museums of the world and I'd point out the da Vinci paintings from their textbooks. In Paris, they could play among the sculptures in Rodin's garden. Fruit bats would poop on their heads in Sydney's botanical garden. We could dip our toes in every ocean in the world. *You want pizza? Let's get it in Napoli.* I would show them that I could be a mom and also work, and that the loneliness of the female singer and musician, caught in a man's world, was a thing of the past.

But Brad had the parental right to say no, and he decided that if he couldn't be there, our sons wouldn't be there either— even on a trip as short as two days. He claimed that I had killed his music career by leaving him and insisted that there was no way he could make a living in Montreal because he didn't speak French. When anyone suggested that he spend time working in New York if Montreal was the problem, he said that he would never leave his children with me, even to work. Since Brad had stopped making money, I was fully responsible for supporting him and the kids. The only way I could do that was to tour, which meant going without seeing my children for long stretches. Brad also refused to leave the house I had inherited from my mother. I was back to sleeping on Ariel's couch again.

After our separation, I became really uncomfortable if I ran into him, and constantly looked behind me or scanned the sidewalks ahead of me so that I could spot him in enough time that I could turn down another street. I peered through shop windows to make sure he wasn't inside before I went in. I was a mess. We shared custody fifty-fifty, and when the boys came to me for my week, Francis wouldn't let me touch him and Arc distanced himself in other ways. I begged for help from lawyers, the school authorities, and therapists, but there wasn't much they could do. After a while, no matter the financial pressure I was under, I couldn't keep touring. I needed to stay put in Montreal and regain the trust of my kids.

Today, we are still in the middle of it, so this story isn't over. But there is no point in talking too much more about my troubles with Brad. If the kids ever read this book, it's important that I don't trash their dad. They need to believe in him and they deserve to love him. I, too, had loved Brad. I keep saying that to myself. I married him and had two kids with him and I was in my right mind, so I also have to ask myself how it all got so bad. I made my bed and I will sleep in it, but I will never understand how it got so bad.

When we were together, Brad and I connected most through music, but even there he made me feel like a failure. He always said that he "made" my career. He described me as being in the gutter when he met me, and claimed that he was the one who discovered that I was a great talent. I guess he needs to believe that. But I had been "discovered" before him by all sorts of people, Nick Hill being the most important to me, and I had already put out a couple of EPs and had toured a lot. As I've said, Brad thought I didn't work hard enough. He was right in that I didn't live for my work and was not driven by visions of fame or money. I wanted to be an artist *and* a mother *and* a wife. Once the children came along, they are what I cared about most. Brad has said that I was a bad wife, and told me that it was my fault that Arc was born so premature—something hugely painful to me. But looking back on it now, I can see that neither of those things was true.

After the divorce was final, a judge ordered him out of the house on Querbes. It was freeing to be out of the relationship, but mostly terrifying. I hadn't lived alone in fifteen years. I missed the kids badly when they were with Brad, in an apartment two blocks away from me, so on his custody weeks I worked as much as possible. I was devastated when my mom died, and totally freaked out when Arc was born so early, but the loss and agony I felt over my divorce and the separation from my kids was way beyond either of those experiences.

At night when I was alone, I'd blast music and dance. I'd travel through the house with a glass of wine in my hand and a smoke hanging out of my mouth just to see if I still liked smoking. I'd go into the different rooms and sit on the empty beds. I'd open boxes that hadn't been opened in years and make different piles on the floor: Kate and Anna archive, Martha archive, kids' drawings. I'd put my babies' clothes into bags to go to Goodwill but couldn't seem to get the bags out the door. I was so lonely, I thought about adopting a child, then thought maybe a dog would be a better idea, but in the end I didn't adopt a dog either. I didn't shop or cook but ate what I could scavenge from the fridge—wilted radicchio, a heel of cheese, some stale crackers, the last of the spicy olives. I never wanted this. I never wanted to have a broken home.

I wiped the tears from my face and told myself it would get better. I made sure to leave some wine in the bottle before I went to bed. Sometimes I'd stay in the guest room downstairs instead of sleeping in my own bed. Everyone said it *would* get better. "You had no choice," I told myself. "This is the way it has to be."

It's Saturday. On Mondays, I get the kids back. I've vacuumed and cleaned their room. I've done all the laundry and their drawers are full of clean clothes. The fridge is empty, but I'll do a big shop tomorrow and have the food delivered. It's almost September and we'll soon have to figure out where the school bus will drop Arc off and pick him up: some corner between our two homes? This sucks. I wasn't prepared for this.

My hair is turning gray but I'm going to leave it. I did a show last night and I was amazing. At least two men are texting me who want me to be their girlfriend, but I turn my phone off. I'm not anywhere near ready for that, although I have been a bit of a slut. Making up for lost time, I guess.

Sometimes I dream about Brad. About kissing him, about his body, about his smile. But when I see him on the street, I want to turn away.

When I started writing this book, nothing really bad had

happened. Then it was finished, and I thought I'd described the worst that could happen, and then came the divorce and the abrupt end to the dream I had of how we were going to live.

It's important for me to get off this subject. Good things come out of bad things. This I know to be true. I still have hopes and dreams and, as much as possible, that is where my eyes are cast. It seems dismal right now, but I'll tell you a change is gonna happen.

I'm a fucking phoenix or, if you prefer, a Hydra. Shit's gonna get a lot fucking better. I'm not sick, my kids aren't sick, we live in a great town, and I am capable of making money to survive.

I'm a fucking Hydra.

You bite my head off and I come back.

Nineteen

I SPENT A COUPLE OF YEARS IN total darkness. Bawling in the flies of theaters, suffocating my sobs in the curtains as I watched Rufus sing "Both Sides Now" as if it had been written for me. Turning my face away from the kids so they wouldn't see me cry after they were mean to me, following their father's script. Lighting candles and crossing myself in churches all over the world just in case it might help. Pleading with and paying lawyers in hopes that they could fix an unfixable situation. From the evidence, I figured I was unworthy of love and that I would be single for the rest of my life.

Then a man walked in, not particularly tall, once upon a time dark but now gray and exceedingly handsome, and he changed everything. He didn't make Brad change his ways and he didn't get me my kids back full-time, but he made life much easier to live and opened my eyes to things they had been closed to, maybe for my whole life.

His name is Nico, and when he changed my orbit in May 2018, I'd never experienced spring that way before. I'm shy to tell you how it felt, but I want to try because it's important. Love is important. The lonely winter nights had pulled me down into a place I had never experienced. I was not truly suicidal, but at times I was so sad, I was drawn to the river; jumping in seemed the least brutal and simplest solution to the mess of my life. I'd been in love before Nico—many times, really—but there was always something wrong with me, with them, or with the circumstance. I'd been searching for true love and affection since I was a teenager, and now, in my forties, it came to me. I'd had so little experience with it, I am lucky I even recognized it.

I was participating in my brother's show at St. Ann's Warehouse, a performance space in Brooklyn, the last stop of a tour Rufus had put together called "Northern Stars." He and a small band were covering an array of great songs by Canadian artists: Joni Mitchell, Neil Young, Luc Plamondon, Leonard, Kate and Anna, and others. Because Rufus tends to get squirmy whenever I sing for too long, he'd asked me to do just a couple of numbers, but I was proud to have been asked at all. The competition between me and Rufus onstage had become pretty adoring by this point, and if I still spent my downtime stalking the backstage and drinking the wine that he wasn't going to drink, it was because my feelings of jealousy or envy had waned. Right? (They only survive at all because I love him so much and wish I could be more like him.)

On this tour, though, I told Rufus I didn't want to sing backup and insisted that since he, too, is a great Canadian artist, I wanted to do one of *his* most incredible songs, "Going to a Town." This made him happy. At each performance, I took my time with it, creating a dramatic (some might say overly dramatic) interpretation. The audience seemed to like it, though, and I was showered with compliments as I often am at Rufus's shows; people understandably feel the need to make the little sister feel good. Rufus, in turn, covered one of mine, "Far Away," which I was honored to hear him sing alongside such songs as "So Long, Marianne," "Harvest," "A Case of You," and "(Talk to Me of) Mendocino."

Since my separation, I had lost fifteen pounds from sadness. A few weeks earlier, in LA, I had splurged at Fred Segal on a halter-topped silk animal-print jumpsuit with loose pant legs, and that was how I felt: thin, flailing, unhinged, barely dressed, hungry, and feral. After the show, I slept with someone who everybody in the world wants to sleep with, and I left his giant house the next morning with a pounding headache and a big smile on my face, glad to know that rock 'n' roll was still alive and I was still a part of it.

But, really, I threw myself at people because I was lost and hurt and sad. Many responded, which surprised me. I was always under the impression that men didn't desire me, but it turned out my image of myself was skewed. I'm not saying that I am a great beauty or that I was a delicate bird kept locked in a cage by her former husband. I was just unaware of any possibility that I could be desired by someone I desired back. I was everyone's friend. Their loud, quirky, nice friend. And I think it's true that because I was not an obvious target of men's desire, I was able to develop very strong and loving relationships with men that were sisterly, even when I wanted them to be more.

Ariel and I were talking recently about how different our experiences as women have been. She was, and still is, so attractive that everybody wanted her, and she knew it and allowed herself to be objectified. Often her boyfriends were much older than she was, drawn by her youth and beauty. I can understand, given that I was also in love with her and also desired her and made her the subject of photo projects of mine for school. Now that she's older, she says people don't "see" her as much. She feels invisible and she's not used to it.

I spent twenty-five years prancing around onstage in high heels and fun outfits, and that is where I was seen, and even adored, by some. But when I got offstage and put on my lumberjack shirt and sneakers, I faded away, turning into another one of the guys hanging out with the band. I don't want to say Brad didn't ever love me, because he did, but he never seemed happy about it. Instead he seemed burdened. (Now I realize that maybe he just felt guilty.) Male adulation is not the most important thing in the life of a woman, and I don't want it to seem that I can't exist without the love of a man, but love and compassion and trust in a relationship are important. Can I live without love? Of course. And before that night at St. Ann's, I had been expecting to do just that, live my life alone and be a mother to my sons.

I'd actually met Nico ten years earlier. He'd done some work on our big house in Brooklyn with Phil. A gifted carpenter and builder, he and Phil had been friends for years, and Phil also spoke of him often. I was a new mom with a house to renovate at the time, so I guess I just never really clocked him. Then I ran into him a couple of times in the year before the St. Ann's show and saw what I had failed to notice a decade earlier, which is how beautiful he is. But I also noticed he had a girl-friend. This time, though, when I met him backstage after the show, he was alone. I asked him where his girlfriend was, and he told me that they had broken up. I told him that I wasn't sad to hear it and asked him to call me. The next day, he did.

A week later, I drove down from Montreal to see him at his little house in Woodstock. I arrived late at night and he was waiting for me on the veranda. I rolled down my window and he leaned in and kissed me. That was that; it was as if a deal had been sealed between us that read, "I think I could love you." The visit stretched for days. I became a person I didn't recognize, as if my body was being born again. My vision expanded and my breath got deeper and quieter. I doubt he'd appreciate me telling you this. He's not a blabber like me, but I can't help saying how deeply I fell in love with him.

At the time, Nico was working with Phil on a jobsite in Woodstock. At first, we didn't tell anyone we were together. While he was at work, I lounged on the big bed in his slightly shabby but incredibly charming apartment as if I were a queen, listening to the perfect pitch of spring in Woodstock. The trees were in full, shocking blossom. There were flowers everywhere, even punching out from cracks in busy town sidewalks filled with hippies knocking on bongos and still wearing tie-dye after all these years. I would put on sunglasses to protect my eyes against the sheer volume of the tie-dye and steal down to the store, wearing a large hat and not much else, to get us something for dinner and then head right back to our little nest. I painted my nails to match the tie-dye, because that's how I felt, and shaved my legs and fixed my hair. I cried tears of joy because I wasn't afraid anymore of the power that Brad had over when I could see the children or what they would be saying when they came home to me, or of the emails and texts I kept getting from him about how I was a disgusting person and a bad mother, or of him glaring at me on the street and sometimes even flipping me the bird from his car. All of that faded away in the little bungalow apartment at the end of a cul-de-sac in Woodstock. The affection, tenderness, and sheer amount of lovemaking between Nico and me was more powerful than the fear, sadness, and endless manipulation of my divorce.

Of course, I had to go home: I longed for the kids. But I drove back to Woodstock from Montreal every other week for several months. Around that time, someone had given me Van Morrison's old *Veedon Fleece* album, and I turned it up as I drove, his voice and poetry reverberating in me with added meaningfulness as he sang about laying it down for a while and taking a rest, hidden away from the world. (I still love that goddamn record, even though the man himself is a real schmuck who once, after I opened a show for him in Toronto, came on to me in a way that was not only sexist and boorish but uninteresting and sad. So different from his music.)

* * *

I was in love, but still had to keep on dealing with disentangling from Brad. Soon, in one of the endless hearings I endured, the judge ordered that Brad and I sell our house in Brooklyn in order to split the assets.

With a lot of emotional and physical help from Nico, I took care of everything, which with five floors of stories to pack up and clear out, was quite an undertaking. I would drive down from Montreal for a few days at a time to work at it. I packed what I could and what mattered to me, but Brad was unwilling to get involved. We couldn't be in the same room at this point, let alone agree on how to dismantle our communal property. I had neighbors come in and take what they wanted, then put heaps of books, clothes, blankets, dishes, and furniture on the curb, where they were soon picked up. The moldy, dusty stuff in the basement took three Got Junk truckloads to remove. Nico helped, which made me feel a little guilty because he had better things to do, but it also meant a lot that we were doing this work of dismantling my marriage together.

I finally started to grow the thick skin that my therapists recommended, though it's still not a skin I feel comfortable in. The house had to go, and I didn't regret it. When the sale closed, I got two checks and sent one to Brad and it was over.

Nico moved to Montreal during the summer after we met. At first, he stayed at Ariel's and then he moved into my guest room—we were being so discreet because I was worried about how the boys would react to their mother having a boyfriend. But they liked Nico, and Nico liked them back. I also think the idea of having two adults in the house appealed to their concept of what a normal family is. Nico never tried to be their dad—that wouldn't have gone down well. But he did start to take care of them, and Arc and Francis seemed to enjoy being able to play sports and build things and run around outside for hours with another male figure, a man their mother loved and who loved her back.

Before Nico arrived in our lives, there was so much emotion around the divorce that things could get out of hand, with the children screaming at me and hitting and kicking at me or each other. I lost it completely a couple of times with Arc, and the shock of it made me so depressed, I would end up in tears and the kids would be in tears and we would all roll up into a ball on the floor, hugging, kissing, and apologizing. With Nico there to balance things, we got into a much better rhythm, even though the children were still sad that their parents weren't together and a lot of very surprising remarks continued to come out of their mouths, especially during the first day or two of "Mom's weeks." I learned quickly, with the help of professionals, to let things go—the little things that bothered me, and the big things, too.

My kids are big, strong, loud, and physical, and sometimes they are out of control. Their rooms are messy, they aren't much when it comes to doing chores, and they say some bad words. But so what? Sometimes it's better to just throw a ball or draw together or watch a movie, even though I want every moment with them to be about reading or playing music or learning a new skill or having a philosophical discussion. I want them to be ready to achieve their dreams. I worry about them when they're at their dad's—there's a lot of screen time and video games and pizza and candy—and it makes me upset, but then I remember what I was like as a kid. My homework was rarely done perfectly. I said bad words. I was angry with my parents. I acted out. I recently found my sixth-grade report card and it's terrible. (I did not show it to Arc.)

Sometimes, still, our home life gets so challenging I ask Nico if he wants to go back to Woodstock where his life was easier and he was free of all this drama. He always says no, that he loves me and the boys and that we will find a way.

When the money from the sale of the house came in, I wanted to do something that I had been dreaming of for years: a big project, a labor of love. And I did it—well, *we* did it. I bought a slightly dilapidated old building in the Mile End neighborhood of Montreal in which I would open a music space/café/bar/community center/clubhouse/gallery and anything else I could think of.

URSA was born.

The word *ursa* had been rattling around in my brain for a couple of years. It is the name of the female bear constellations (Ursa Major and Ursa Minor, or the Big Dipper and Little Dipper). One day when I was particularly down, my friend Melissa had put a copper bracelet around my wrist with the words *Mama Bear* engraved on it, hoping it would give me strength. I took it as a sign. I drew *Mama Bear* on different parts of my body, wondering whether I would finally follow through and get a tattoo, but no, the ballpoint ink sufficed. I was a mama bear who felt (and still feels) as though my cubs had been taken away from me, but that I still had to keep Arc and Francis safe and healthy, even from a distance.

URSA encapsulated that concern and married it to the idea of a venue/café that had been kicking around in my head for years. This is the start of the original URSA manifesto:

> University of Radical Symbolic Associations
> United Rendering of Surface Accolades
> Usual Rampant Sensual Artists
> Uninvited Rancor Salvation Arts
> Usurped by Reckless Serpentine Apes
> Universe of Rather Similar Arses…
> URSA is whatever you want it to be.

The manifesto went on to describe a project that no person in their right mind would ever invest in. But plenty of people wanted to be a part of it, or at least watch me and Nico try to make it happen.

Lucky for me, Nico can make and fix anything. He also has the instinct to reuse and repurpose, which fit the budget—after buying the building, there was no money left and not much coming in, because I had slowed down so I could be home more for the kids. Nico built the counters and the stage from old tables. We bought secondhand appliances from Goodwill and accepted donations of pots and pans and dishes.

My cousins Sylvan and Lily, Vinnie and Kathleen, along with friends and people from the neighborhood, rolled up their sleeves to help. We held meetings where I presented lists of what I thought needed to be done (based on what, I'm not sure), and people raised their hands to volunteer and took items on. I made giant pots of soup and opened many bottles of wine to keep them working. None of us had any experience at this kind of thing, but we jumped in and did it.

On May 20, 2019, two months after I bought the building, we had our first event, a fundraiser. I made dinner for our fifty guests—Kate's borscht, homemade gravlax, and spring lamb. Rufus was in town and he and I did a set of music, and the family joined in. Some local artists had donated works and I auctioned them off in my apron, between slinging drinks, serving food, and singing songs.

It was the beginning of something beautiful, audacious, financially stupid, and full-time. It started off as a type of clubhouse designed to keep me home more and be a center for music and art for all ages, and quickly grew into a well-liked, great-sounding small music venue. In the months that followed, we booked dozens of bands and made brunches and baked bread, put on exhibits, hosted art lessons, exercise classes, and club nights, and ran a kids' camp.

When the pandemic locked everyone down in March 2020, I was honestly kind of happy to stop. I also had been writing songs and had begun making an album, and was glad to be able to focus on that. But after a couple of months of being closed, I started to worry about how we would survive or ever even open again.

As I write this, we are getting ready to reopen URSA. I will put my apron back on and start organizing the kids' camp and some shows. It will be a while before things are back to what they were. If ever. We put so much work into URSA, and I want to see it thriving again. But I am not an entrepreneur and club owner. I am a singer-songwriter, and with this new record I made, soon I will be returning to that and going out on the road to promote it. I love the road—in the past, it's been the thing that I have loved the most—but now I'm dreading having to negotiate the schedule with my ex and working extra hard to keep the trust of the boys. But the boys also need to know that their mom can work, and I need to support them. I know that sounds simple, but at this point I can only think in simple terms. If I try to control the situation or even try to understand why it got so hard, I won't get out of bed.

When I look back, I know I have gotten less crazy over the years. One way I can tell is by remembering my reaction to Nan Goldin's photo series *The Ballad of Sexual Dependency*, which I flipped through on my phone a few years ago after she asked me to sing at an event marking the thirtieth anniversary of her debut exhibition of the images. The photos reminded me of my life in New York. Times I spent with Rufus and his friends in gay bars and at the Chelsea Hotel. Times I spent with Phil and Mercedes and Reuben, dabbling in drugs and weaving in and out of bars and rock clubs in the East Village.

I'm sometimes surprised I'm even here. I could have so easily died. I could have been the subject of a similar photo montage of excess and complete collapse. A part of me misses being on my bathroom floor with blisters on my feet from walking home for miles in heels. I miss strangers' mouths on mine; I miss the taste of cigarettes and making out with girls. But I also know I want to live a long time. I want to be there for my sons and for Nico, and that means I have to give all that up in order to be healthy and functioning. I need to make money for my family and to chisel at the stone to create an image of myself that works for the long haul.

Still, when I saw Nan's photos of youthful debauchery, with all those beautiful people, I wanted to crawl inside them. They aren't the usual magazine images of sexy, pretty young things, posed and primped for the shot. They're pictures of people in ecstasy, pain, joy, boredom, shame, and loneliness, their bodies oozing desire and fear you can practically smell. I know that smell.

But I have learned to be more responsible. In truth, though I know this memoir gives the impression that I've lived a life of excess, I've always been solid, and I get more and more solid with time. A few years ago I tried to get a prescription for an antidepressant and the psychiatrist said no because he thought I was coping quite well, considering. I've always exercised and eaten well and kept my finances in some semblance of order. I'm terrible at folding laundry, yes, but I dust regularly and I'm a good cook. I'm on the kids' butts about their homework and have even been asked to sit on the PTA. Still, once in a while, I still find myself in a taxicab at six in the morning, laughing my tits off.

Epilogue

NOTHING REALLY BAD HAS HAPPENED YET.

That sentence haunts me. When I started working on this book, it ran through my mind over and over. Was it wishful thinking? Why did I keep coming back to it?

After Aunt Teddy read an early draft, I told her about the sentence and she thought it was strange, too. Hadn't plenty of bad-enough things happened to me?

I replied, "Exactly. I will write that nothing bad has happened yet and then I will describe some bad things and that will be kinda funny. Right?"

She wasn't convinced. Neither was I, really, but the idea kept running through my mind.

I finally figured out why when I was reading a novel by Miriam Toews, *All My Puny Sorrows*, while trying to stay away from Anderson Cooper and the other pundits on CNN, and I came across the sentence: "The words 'nothing bad has happened yet,' a lyric from a Loudon Wainwright song, knocked around in my head…"

Goddamn it! I sat up in bed and racked my brain, saying the line out loud, and then it came to me in Loudon's sweet, high, perfect melodic voice, "Nothing bad has happened yet," followed by him sing-speaking in a lower register, "and everyone is happy." It's from a song of his called "Thanksgiving" on a record called *Therapy*, and refers to a photograph, or a time, really, when everything was okay in my father's family—my family.

In the song, he describes going down for his afternoon nap, something he still takes daily (like a two-year-old), and having a dream about his family:

Mother and Father, both still young
And naturally they love us
We're all lying on a lawn at night
Watching the stars above us
Lord, every year we gather here
To eat around this table
Give us the strength to stomach as much
As fast as we are able

As someone who has made a lot of Thanksgiving dinners in my time, that's not exactly the sentiment you hope for. Earlier in the song, Loudon describes the meal, no doubt slaved over by the women in the family, as tasteless. But really what I hear in his lyric is some regret and a whole lot of sadness. A wish that it could have worked out better.

My father drove me to the beach on Shelter Island, when I was fifteen and he was the age I am now, to tell me that I'd get through whatever agony I was feeling and things would be all right. We looked up at the stars together. One time in

London, in the middle of the night, I found him waiting up for me in his boxers when I crept in way too late, so he could tell me—or maybe he was asking me—that he couldn't have done fatherhood differently, that he had to work, and play gigs, and make money, and that is how he supported us, his family. He said he didn't know *how* to do it differently. He experienced his children through the lens of songwriting and reluctantly created a line of self-absorbed songwriters. Oh joy!

But in truth, he was not the originator of this particular family legacy. Anyone who knows about Loudon Wainwright III knows about Loudon Wainwright Jr. and his monthly *Life* magazine column, "The View from Here," so confessional, reflective, and personal. Junior's own father had died when he was seventeen, and in a column titled "The Sum of Recollection Just Keeps Growing," which appeared thirty years after Loudon Sr.'s death, my grandfather described the moment when his uncle handed him his father's obituary to review and "the raw facts of my father's name and death seemed so utterly unconnected to the powerful, demanding, volatile person who had been such a huge part of my life." He also admitted that he was still searching for evidence of his father's love, and that he'd recently found it in some home movies Senior had shot, in the way his dad had held the camera as he filmed his son skating, the way the camera jerked when he saw the little boy fall and went toward him. "Even if we're late we can still reach out for fathers...," Loudon Jr. wrote, "and find good moments in what they left behind."

What did my own father mean when he wrote that nothing bad had happened yet? That his parents were not yet divorced? That the family house had not yet caught on fire (which it did, and almost killed everyone)? That his own divorce hadn't happened yet? That his children were with him in his dreams?

My family is a broken family whose members hang on tight to each other nonetheless. We fight, but we make up relatively quickly. We try not to hold grudges, but it's hard not to. Rufus has done some therapy with Loudon in an attempt to fix their relationship, but I think their breakthroughs are distilled by what they say in their songs.

Both Rufus and I now live in our own broken families. It feels almost inevitable. My children blame me for breaking up our home, but maybe one day they'll realize I had no choice. Or even better, they won't care. Sometimes I think they would do better shipped off to a wonderful boarding school, so they don't have to navigate their parents' polarized homes and hearts. But then again, all I want is to be near them. Having access to my kids only half the time is, and will always be, my personal tragedy. It is by far the hardest thing for me to cope with.

When I'm not with them, I avoid going outside sometimes. When I walk by parks filled with kids or hear kids playing in the schoolyard, I wonder where the boys are and what they are doing. I know it's a sacrifice I made. And it's getting a little easier, but still when I travel and see kids at the airport or on foreign city streets, I drop my head so as not to stare.

Music will save me as it always has. I keep thinking of the record *The McGarrigle Hour*. On it are the family and our closest friends—Chaim and Emmylou, Lily and Sylvan. People I've known my whole life. It has a version of us all singing "School Days," a song from Loudon's first record, and Lily sings Gaby's favorite song, "Alice Blue Gown," which my grandmother sang to us in her nightgown on many a fun Saturday night. There is Anna and Chaim singing "Young Love" as if they were made for each other and living out a romantic tragedy. There is "Year of the Dragon," the first song I ever recorded for an album (which some people still think is my best).

But the track I find the most moving is the only recording of me and Rufus with both our parents, singing "What'll I Do." It is a love song that is a wish for a lost love and so sad it feels fitting for a funeral. When I listen to it, I need to climb into bed because it always hits me so hard.

I can't listen to it any longer today. It's another Monday and I get the kids back in a few hours. I have to wipe away the tears and make dinner for their sake, and my own. I don't want them to see me sad. I want them to know how happy I am and how grateful I am to be alive.

This book has been a thorn in my side for almost seven years. I have written it and rewritten it several times over. I have given it several introductions, epilogues, and even a eulogy. I abandoned it regularly and tried to completely kill it. I've burned copies and used the backs of pages as scrap paper on which I taught my kids addition and subtraction. An early draft was used as evidence against me in my divorce case and, after that, I didn't touch the manuscript for two years. I gave back my first advance, but then took another one because I needed the money.

But I'm glad I did and, in case you're wondering, I do not regret telling you my story.

Despite my newfound happiness, I am still shocked by life's blows. In 2017, I drove to Syracuse from Montreal to meet Phil at the hospital to see Nick Hill, who had suffered a massive stroke and lost the ability to walk and talk. He's since learned to walk again but most likely will never talk. He's aware of what is going on around him and is in many respects the same person he has always been: interested in things, loving, vibrant, and passionate. But I miss his beautiful voice and words.

Then, in the spring of 2020, Hal Willner died after contracting COVID, another man crucial to so many artists' careers, so creative and giving, and who had been a father figure to me.

In September that year, the person who believed in me the most, our rock, Aunt Teddy, died a tedious death. Though she had been declining for years, she was not ready to go, and she was angry and afraid at the end, as well as in pain. Luckily, her life partner, best friend, and ex-husband, Richard, Jack's father, was there to hold her. But soon after, he, too, died of a stroke and lay for days alone on the floor of his apartment.

Because of the pandemic, I've had little real contact with my family and friends in the United States. I miss my brother, but we will see each other soon. My father has been on Shelter Island, growing a beard like Mr. Natural's and enjoying his life. Though we love each other very much, it's always been from a distance, so this last stretch felt more or less normal, although sad. I wish we could have done better. When the borders open, I want to go on a long road trip to see Nick and Alex in Ithaca, Phil in Woodstock, and other old friends along the way. I want to bring the kids west to see Rufus and Viva and Jörn. I should start with my dad. We can go to a restaurant and I'll try not to be late.

Soon, I will get on planes once more and go places and stand in front of audiences and sing my new songs and see the other people I've been missing.

If I'm lucky, I'm about halfway through my life. Perhaps I am someone whose luck gets better halfway through. That would be good.

Acknowledgments

I would like to thank everyone named in this book for showing me who I am.

But there are a handful of people who helped me through the telling of these stories whom I need to thank specifically. Of these, Danny Goldberg has been the most important. I don't think I truly expected to finish the memoir or have it be published. The fact that he kept insisting I write it and encouraging me to keep going has made it possible. Another very instrumental person is Laura Nolan, my agent, who did not abandon me after I made it practically impossible for her to do her job. I would also like to thank Anne Collins, my editor, for ironing out the kinks and making me see what works and what doesn't. She kept my voice but also made it better.

I'm also grateful to Whitney Frick, who wrestled with an early version; to my good friend Kathryn Jezer-Morton, who read through it on several occasions and gave solid advice; and to Ben Schafer at Hachette Books, for his encouragement and guidance; as well as to Peter Wark at management for his attention to detail and hard work.

I'm thankful to Nico, too, for his support and help in pushing it over the finishing line. Without him I would not have believed in myself enough to continue. I am also grateful to him for his preparation and service of "café au lit," given most of this book was written in bed.

There are many things that I was not at liberty to say, but I know that I have also said plenty and perhaps at my own expense. I have not dedicated this book to my children because it is mostly about a time before they were born and my struggles with things I don't want them to have to be concerned with. But I will say that everything I do is for them.

As I sit here in my bed trying to finish this, I mean really finish it, I can't help but shed a tear for my mother and hope that she likes it.